Brand-Name
DIABETIC MEALS
IN MINUTES

**Quick and healthy
recipes to make your
meals tastier and
your life easier**

American
Diabetes
Association®

Book Acquisitions	Susan Reynolds
Production Director	Carolyn R. Segree
Production Coordinator	Peggy M. Rote
Editor	Sherrye Landrum
Designer/Desktop Publishing	Harlowe Typography, Inc.
Cover Design	Wickham & Associates, Inc.

The suggestions and information contained in this publication are generally consistent with the *Clinical Practice Recommendations* and other policies of the American Diabetes Association, but they do not represent the policy or position of the Association or any of its boards or committees. Reasonable steps have been taken to ensure the accuracy of the information presented. However, the American Diabetes Association cannot ensure the safety or efficacy of any product or service described in this publication. Individuals are advised to consult a physician or other appropriate health care professional before undertaking any diet or exercise program or taking any medication referred to in this publication. Professionals must use and apply their own professional judgment, experience, and training and should not rely solely on the information contained in this publication before prescribing any diet, exercise, or medication. The American Diabetes Association—its officers, directors, employees, volunteers, and members—assumes no responsibility or liability for personal or other injury, loss, or damage that may result from the suggestions or information in this publication.

American Diabetes Association
1660 Duke Street
Alexandria, Virginia 22314

Library of Congress Cataloging-in-Publication Data

Brand-name diabetic meals in minutes: quick and healthy recipes to
   make your meals tastier and your life easier.
      p.   cm.
   ISBN 0-945448-76-7 (pbk.)
    1. Diabetes—Diet therapy—Recipes. 2. Brand name products.
  I. American Diabetes Association
  RC662.B72 1997   97–7677
  641.5′6314—dc21   CIP

Table of Contents

Acknowledgments

The recipes in this book were contributed by the following corporate sponsors of the American Diabetes Association. With their support and assistance, the Association is able to pursue research to find a cure and to develop and distribute educational programs and materials to improve the lives of all people affected by diabetes in the meantime.

Those companies that contributed recipes for this volume are

Campbell Soup Company
Kraft Foods, Inc.
The Weetabix Company, Inc.
Benevia (Equal)
Dean Foods
Estee Corporation (The Hain Food Group)
Eskimo Pie

Introduction

Our grandmothers made all their meals from scratch—hot bread at every meal—and there was always a pot of something simmering on the stove. Perhaps our grandmothers had more time than we do now, but we have supermarkets and many more foods to choose from. The supermarket is where we can go for help when we have little time for cooking but still want the great taste of homemade meals. We can buy foods that will give us a head start. Many food products—from chicken broth to frozen entrees—can save us time in the kitchen. It's just a matter of learning how to fit these products into the menus for the day. This cookbook can help.

In this book you will find taste-tested recipes from the kitchens of several corporate sponsors of the American Diabetes Association. The brand name food products in these recipes can give you a head start on tasty, healthy meals. In this book you will also find menu suggestions and a shopping list you can copy and take to the grocery store with you. The more time we can save for you, the easier it will be for you to meet your healthy eating goals each day.

Why is what you choose to eat important?

Every healer since Hippocrates has said that food is our best medicine. We may not be able to buy good health, but we can buy good foods. And "good" foods are the same for everyone! If you have diabetes, you don't need to eat differently from everyone else. In particular, eating well helps you

- gain more control over your blood glucose levels
- keep your blood fats in a healthy range
- keep your blood pressure levels in a healthy range
- lose weight or maintain the weight that's right for you
- enjoy a variety of foods that give you all the nutrients a healthy body needs

You see, food is powerful medicine indeed.

You'll notice from the list above that food affects more than just blood glucose levels. Healthy levels of blood fats and blood pressure are important, too. People with diabetes are more likely to develop heart and blood vessel disease. Cutting back on the amount of fats and oils in your meals and controlling your weight is the best way to keep cholesterol levels within a healthy range. Many of the recipes in this book have been adjusted to give you a lower amount of fat without losing the taste and texture of the dish.

People with diabetes are prone to high blood pressure, so one thing you can do is watch how much sodium is in the foods you eat. Of the sodium in most meals, 1/3 comes from processed food, 1/3 from the salt shaker, and 1/3 occurs naturally in foods. Some of the recipes in this book contain more sodium than usual. These recipes have been flagged with a little salt shaker. You can always cut back on the amount of table salt in a recipe and use more herbs and seasonings for flavor. Salt is not used in the water whenever you cook rice or pasta for any of these recipes.

What else can you do to be healthy?

Hippocrates also said, "Eating well will not, by itself, keep well a person who does not exercise, for food and exercise being opposite in effect, work together to produce health." Eating right and exercising every day help you control your blood sugar, blood fats, and blood pressure. For most people, eating well and exercising daily also bring about weight loss or help you to maintain your weight at a healthy level. Even small weight losses (5–20 pounds) can make a big difference in your blood sugar control. Exercise generally

- causes blood sugar to drop
- burns calories
- reduces stress
- improves the way you feel about yourself
- builds and maintains muscle mass
- improves circulation

That's why exercise helps with all of the special health concerns of people with diabetes. (And of everybody else, too.)

Do you know what to eat?

You should have a meal plan designed for the food you like and to fit your daily schedule and exercise. The best way to find out what to eat is to consult a registered dietitian (RD). The RD can help you develop a meal plan. Your sex, age, weight, and the amount you exercise will influence your calorie needs. The RD can show you serving sizes and help you choose different foods to fit your meal plan. Your RD can help you adjust your meal plan for changes in your schedule and learn to use the Diabetes Food Pyramid or Exchange Lists of foods to plan meals. (Pyramid servings and exchanges are given for each recipe in this book. Optional ingredients are not included in the nutrient analysis.)

The Pyramid and you

If you want an easy way to remember what foods to eat, use the Diabetes Food Pyramid (see page x). It was adapted from the USDA Food Guide Pyramid, and both tell you how to choose your foods for good health.

The pyramid idea is simple. Each day, choose most of your foods from the larger sections of the pyramid on the bottom and a few servings of the foods from the smaller sections on the top. This means that you want to eat more grains, beans, and starchy vegetables than anything else. You add generous helpings of vegetables, and sweeten the day with several pieces of fruit. Servings from these three groups are the foundation of a very healthful pyramid—and good health for you. Sprinkle in a few servings of meat, cheese, or eggs for protein, and 2–3 servings of milk or yogurt each day. You'll notice that sweets, fats, and alcohol are in the point of the pyramid—and for good reason. They can be part of your meal plan, but you should have just a little of each. They contribute very few of the nutrients that your body needs.

Try to eat a wide variety of foods each week. High-fiber foods, such as fruits, vegetables, grains, and beans, fill you up and keep your body working as it should. And you should be aware of how much fat, sugar, and salt are added to your meals.

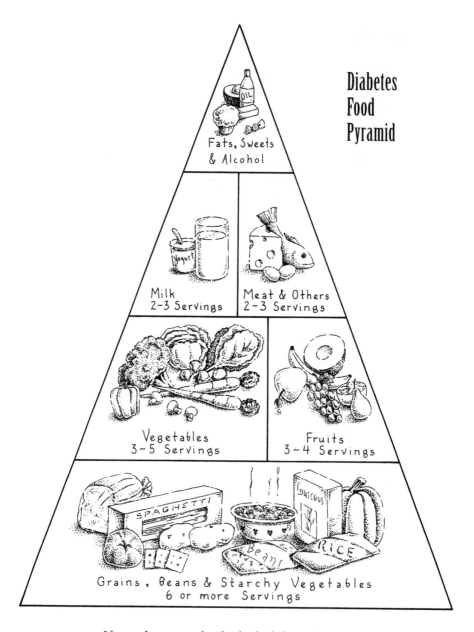

Fats, Sweets & Alcohol

Diabetes Food Pyramid

Milk
2~3 Servings

Meat & Others
2~3 Servings

Vegetables
3~5 Servings

Fruits
3~4 Servings

Grains, Beans & Starchy Vegetables
6 or more Servings

If you choose to drink alcohol, limit the amount to one or two glasses of wine, beer, or whiskey, and always have it with a meal. Alcohol can make your blood glucose drop rapidly, so it is very important that you eat when you drink alcohol. Check with your dietitian or health care provider about a safe amount of alcohol for you.

Does it matter when you eat?

Timing your meals and snacks helps diabetes medications work better and keeps your blood sugar levels from rising or falling drastically. Here are some general guidelines for you:

- Spread meals and snacks evenly throughout the day.
- Eat at about the same times every day.
- Don't skip meals or save foods from one meal for another meal.

One other important tip is: At each meal, try to eat the same amount of food that you ate at that meal the day before. (You don't have to eat the same food, but choose the same number of servings from that food group.) Eating a consistent amount of food makes it easier for you to predict changes in your blood glucose level.

How much should you eat?

This is probably the trickiest part of meal planning and the easiest part to do something about. First, eat all the servings from each food group on your meal plan. Second, weigh or measure your servings. If you don't already have these, get yourself a set of measuring spoons and cups and an inexpensive food scale. You cannot know whether your servings are the right size if you don't measure or weigh them. Eyeballing only works after you practice measuring and eating the correct sizes for a few weeks.

Are these budget-stretching meals?

Any time you do your own cooking at home, you save money. If you use brand name products, you're still saving money over eating in a restaurant or having carry-out food. If you use a lot of one particular product, it may be less expensive to buy larger size containers of that brand. Cooking in large batches and freezing meals to reheat later will save you time and money. Planning your menus to use up the foods you have on hand prevents waste, and that saves you money. Ethnic foods, such as Chinese or Mexican dishes, with a lot of a grain like rice and a little protein—meat, beans, cheese, or eggs—will stretch your dollar, too. And they're right on target with the pyramid way to eat!

How can you change the way you eat now?

Take it one step at a time. Don't try to change the habits of a lifetime in one week. Focus on just one change, for example, eating more grains each day. Over time, try to eat a wider variety of foods. Let your motto be: Try it, you might like it. Experiment with different recipes and foods. You can only benefit from your discoveries.

What about desserts

You can eat sugar. You won't upset your blood glucose levels if you can modify desserts to fit into your meal plan. You could change one ingredient to reduce fat or use sugar substitutes instead of sugar. Or eat a smaller serving.

Tips to try for fitting dessert into your meal plan.

- Eat a smaller portion of your favorite dessert to enjoy the taste you love without overdoing the calories.
- When preparing desserts, use reduced-fat or no-fat substitutes for any sour cream, cream cheese, or whipped toppings.
- Go fruity. Use more fresh fruits as toppings on frozen desserts or puddings.
- You can sweeten fruit and other foods with sugar substitutes in place of table sugar.

In conclusion

Each of us needs to be creative. Preparing the food that you need to eat to live can be a very creative activity. So, get into the kitchen, get creative, and start enjoying your meals from start to finish, just like Granny did.

Shopping List

PANTRY

Rice
- white
- brown
- wild

Other grains
- popcorn
- bulgur wheat
- barley
- couscous
- millet

Cereals
- hot
  - oatmeal
  - wheat germ
- packaged
  - corn flakes
  - raisin bran

Pastas, noodles
- macaroni
- spaghetti noodles
- fettucine noodles

Breads
- whole grains
- bagels
- sourdough
- rolls
- English muffins
- pita

Crackers
- graham crackers
- soda crackers

Snack foods
- pretzels
- baked tortilla chips
- vanilla wafers

Starchy vegetables
- potatoes
- sweet potatoes
- squash
- corn
- peas

Beans, canned and dried
- peas
- lentils
- black beans
- kidney beans
- pinto beans
- black-eyed peas
- chickpeas, garbanzo beans
- baked beans
- refried beans
- vegetarian chili

Vegetables
- canned
  - tomatoes
  - vegetable juice

Fruits
  dried
    raisins
    apricots
    figs
    prunes
  cans or jars, packed in juice
    pineapple
    mandarin oranges
    peaches
    pears
    juice, 100%, no sugar added

Milk
  evaporated skim milk
  nonfat dried milk (refrigerate
  after opening)

Soups
  canned
    fat-free chicken stock
  dry
    bouillon, cubes or granular

Meat and others
canned seafood
  tuna
  salmon
  crabmeat
  clams

Fats
oils
  olive
  canola
  safflower
  sunflower
  non stick cooking spray

Peanut butter

Nuts
  almonds
  pecans
  walnuts
  pine nuts

Olives
Mayonnaise
Salad dressings

Sweets
  sugar
    brown
    white
  sugar substitutes
    Equal
  honey
  maple syrup
  molasses
  jam or preserves
  jelly

Chocolate
Cocoa
Coffee
Tea
Soft drinks
Mineral water

Vinegars
  cider
  red wine
  balsamic
  rice

Mustard
  dijon
Salsa
Catsup
Chutney

Lemon juice
Pickles
Pickle relish
Soy sauce
Tabasco sauce
Worcestershire sauce
Wine, for cooking

Herbs and spices
  basil
  marjoram
  thyme
  oregano
  rosemary

cilantro
cayenne
caraway seed
celery seeds
dill seeds
cinnamon
cumin
ginger
garlic
nutmeg
paprika
chili powder
curry powder

FOR THE FREEZER

Pastas
  cheese raviolis

Pizza to top with vegetables
Waffles

Vegetables
  corn
  broccoli
  lima beans
  green beans
  stew vegetables
  stir-fry vegetables
Fruits
  strawberries
  mixed berries
  peaches

Fruit juices
  apple
  grape
  cranberry
  orange

Meat and Meat Substitutes
  chicken breasts
  fish fillets, unbreaded
  shrimp, unbreaded
  pork tenderloin
  very lean ground beef
  turkey

Frozen desserts
  ice cream, reduced fat
  fruit juice popsicles
  frozen yogurt
  sherbet
  sorbet

Frozen entrees (reduced calorie)
(generally 1 meat, 1 starch,
1 vegetable)
  beef chow mein
  spaghetti and meatballs
  pot pie

FRESH FOODS
(To buy once a week or more often)

Vegetables
  alfalfa sprouts
  carrots
  cucumbers
  onions
  garlic
  green beans
  broccoli
  cabbage
  tomatoes
  potatoes
  sweet potatoes
  celery
  green peppers, red, or orange
  mushrooms

Leafy green vegetables
  kale
  spinach
  Swiss chard
  bok choy

Fruits
  apples
  strawberries
  blueberries
  oranges
  grapefruits
  grapes
  plums
  kiwis
  bananas
  peaches

Milk and yogurt
  skim milk
  yogurt
  sour cream, nonfat or low fat

Meat and others
  lean beef or pork
  lean or extra lean cold cuts or
    hot dogs
  Poultry
    chicken
    ground turkey
  seafood
    Pacific salmon

Tofu

Cheese
  cheddar
  feta
  cottage cheese

Eggs
Vegetable oils
Butter
Sweets

Appetizers, Beverages, and Sauces

Light 'n Tangy Twister
Spicy Hot Refresher
Bloody Eight
Orange-Mustard Sauce
Strawberry Smoothie
Maple-Flavored Syrup
Raspberry Sauce
Orange Jubilee
Fitness Shake
Holiday Eggnog
Russian-Style Tea
Coffee Latte
Mocha Sauce
Fresh Cranberry Relish
Spiced Fruit Butter
Refrigerator Corn Relish
Sassy Sweet and Sour Dressing
Triple-Berry Jam
Caponata (Italian Eggplant Dip)
Low-Salt Chili Sauce
Amelia Island Punch
Fruity Frappe
Shredded Wheat Snack Mix
Deb's Dilly Dip
Cool Raspberry Fruit Dip
White Sangria Splash
Fiesta Nachos
Salsa Onion Dip

LIGHT 'N TANGY TWISTER

SERVING SIZE
3/4 cup

EXCHANGES
Carbohydrate   1/2
Vegetable   1

PYRAMID SERVINGS
Vegetable   1
Fruit   1/2

NUTRITION FACTS
Calories   74
Calories from Fat 2
Fat   0 g
  Saturated Fat   0 g
Cholesterol   0 mg
Sodium   227 mg
Carbohydrate   16 g
  Dietary Fiber   1 g
  Sugars   14 g
Protein   1 g

2 cups	LIGHT 'N TANGY V8 Vegetable Juice or V8 Vegetable Juice
1/3 cup	orange juice
1/4 cup	grapefruit juice
2 tsp	honey

1. In pitcher, combine "V8" juice, orange juice, grapefruit juice, and honey.
2. Pour over ice. If desired, garnish with celery rib.

Makes about 2 1/2 cups
Number of Servings   3

Recipe provided courtesy of Campbell Soup Company.

SPICY HOT REFRESHER

SERVING SIZE
about 3/4 cup

EXCHANGES
PYRAMID SERVINGS
Vegetable   1

NUTRITION FACTS
Calories   21
Calories From Fat   1
Fat   0 g
  Saturated Fat   0 g
Cholesterol   0 mg
Sodium   272 mg
Carbohydrate   4 g
  Dietary Fiber   1 g
  Sugars   3 g
Protein   1 g

1 1/2 cups	SPICY HOT V8 Vegetable Juice
1/2 cup	chopped, seeded, peeled cucumber
1 Tbsp	lime juice
1/4 tsp	chili powder
1 cup	ice cubes

1. In covered blender or food processor, combine "V8" juice, cucumber, lime juice, and chili powder. Blend until smooth. Add ice cubes, one at a time, blending until ice is finely crushed.
2. Serve immediately.

Makes about 2 1/2 cups
Number of Servings   3

Recipe provided courtesy of Campbell Soup Company.

BLOODY EIGHT

SERVING SIZE
3/4 cup

EXCHANGES
PYRAMID SERVINGS
Vegetable   2

NUTRITION FACTS
Calories   39
Calories from Fat   1
Fat   0 g
  Saturated Fat   0 g
Cholesterol   0 mg
Sodium   482 mg*
Carbohydrate   9 g
  Dietary Fiber   1 g
  Sugars   6 g
Protein   1 g

3 cups	V8 Vegetable Juice
1 tsp	prepared horseradish
1 tsp	Worcestershire sauce
1/2 tsp	hot pepper sauce

1. In pitcher, combine "V8" juice, horseradish, Worcestershire sauce, and hot pepper sauce.
2. Pour over ice. If desired, garnish with celery stick.

Makes about 3 cups
Number of Servings   4

* >400 mg of sodium

Recipe provided courtesy of Campbell Soup Company.

ORANGE-MUSTARD SAUCE

SERVING SIZE
2 Tbsp

EXCHANGES
Carbohydrate   1

PYRAMID SERVINGS
Sweet   1

NUTRITION FACTS
Calories   57
Calories from Fat   1
Fat   0 g
   Saturated Fat   0 g
Cholesterol   0 mg
Sodium   112 mg
Carbohydrate   15 g
   Dietary Fiber   0 g
   Sugars   11 g
Protein   0 g

1 cup	V8 Vegetable Juice
1/2 cup	orange marmalade
1 Tbsp	Dijon-style mustard

1. In 1/2-qt saucepan, combine "V8" juice, marmalade, and mustard. Over medium-high heat, heat to boiling. Reduce heat to low; cook 10 minutes or until sauce thickens, stirring often.
2. Use sauce to baste chicken, pork chops, or turkey cutlets during the last few minutes of broiling or grilling.

Makes about 1 cup sauce
Number of Servings   8

Recipe provided courtesy of Campbell Soup Company.

STRAWBERRY SMOOTHIE

SERVING SIZE
3/4 cup

EXCHANGES
Carbohydrate   1

PYRAMID SERVINGS
Fruit   1/2
Milk   1/2

NUTRITION FACTS
Calories   76
Calories from Fat   1
Fat   0 g
  Saturated Fat   0 g
Cholesterol   2 mg
Sodium   54 mg
Carbohydrate   16 g
  Dietary Fiber   2 g
  Sugars   14 g
Protein   4 g

1 (8 oz)	carton plain nonfat yogurt
1/4 cup	skim milk
1 tsp	EQUAL Measure or 3 packets EQUAL sweetener or 2 Tbsp EQUAL Spoonful
3 cups	frozen strawberries
1 cup	ice cubes

Combine yogurt, milk, and EQUAL in blender container. With blender running, add berries, a few at a time, through opening in lid. Blend until smooth. Add ice cubes one at a time through opening in lid, blending until slushy. Pour into glasses.

Number of Servings   4

MAPLE-FLAVORED SYRUP

SERVING SIZE
1 Tbsp

EXCHANGES
PYRAMID SERVINGS
Free Food

NUTRITION FACTS
Calories   17
Calories from Fat   7
Fat   1 g
  Saturated Fat   0 g
Cholesterol   0 mg
Sodium   9 mg
Carbohydrate   3 g
  Dietary Fiber   0 g
  Sugars   2 g
Protein   0 g

1 cup	apple juice
2 1/2 tsp	cornstarch
1 Tbsp	margarine
1 3/4	tsp EQUAL Measure or 6 packets EQUAL sweetener or 1/4 cup EQUAL Spoonful
1 tsp	maple flavoring
1 tsp	vanilla

1. Combine apple juice and cornstarch in small saucepan. Cook and stir until thickened and bubbly. Cook and stir 2 minutes more. Remove from heat.
2. Stir in margarine, EQUAL, maple flavoring, and vanilla. Serve over pancakes, waffles, or French toast.

Makes 1 cup
Number of Servings   16

RASPBERRY SAUCE

SERVING SIZE
1/4 cup

EXCHANGES
PYRAMID SERVINGS
Fruit   1/2

NUTRITION FACTS
Calories   37
Calories from Fat   3
Fat   0 g
  Saturated Fat   0 g
Cholesterol   0 mg
Sodium   0 mg
Carbohydrate   9 g
  Dietary Fiber   4 g
  Sugars   5 g
Protein   1 g

2 cups	fresh raspberries or thawed frozen unsweetened raspberries
1 Tbsp	orange juice
1 1/4 tsp	EQUAL Measure or 4 packets EQUAL sweetener or 3 Tbsp EQUAL Spoonful
1/2 tsp	finely grated orange peel

1. Place raspberries in blender container; blend until smooth. Strain through sieve; discard seeds. Stir orange juice, EQUAL, and orange peel into puréed berries.
2. Serve over fresh fruit, frozen yogurt, or cheesecake.

Makes 1 cup
Number of Servings   4

ORANGE JUBILEE

SERVING SIZE
4 oz (1/2 cup)

EXCHANGES
PYRAMID SERVINGS
Fruit   1
Milk, skim   1/2

NUTRITION FACTS
Calories   93
Calories from Fat   2
Fat   0 g
  Saturated Fat   0 g
Cholesterol   2 mg
Sodium   48 mg
Carbohydrate   19 g
  Dietary Fiber   0 g
  Sugars   18 g
Protein   4 g

1 small	can (6 oz) frozen orange juice concentrate
2 1/4 cups	skim milk
1/2 tsp	vanilla
1 3/4 tsp	EQUAL Measure or 6 packets EQUAL sweetener or 1/4 cup EQUAL Spoonful
8	ice cubes
	Ground nutmeg or cinnamon (optional)

1. Process orange juice concentrate, milk, vanilla, and EQUAL in food processor or blender until smooth; add ice cubes and process again until smooth.
2. Serve in small glasses; sprinkle with nutmeg or cinnamon, if desired.

Number of Servings   6

FITNESS SHAKE

SERVING SIZE
8 oz (1 cup)

EXCHANGES
PYRAMID SERVINGS
Starch   1/2
Fruit   1
Milk, skim   1

NUTRITION FACTS
Calories   188
Calories from Fat   14
Fat   2 g
  Saturated Fat   0 g
Cholesterol   4 mg
Sodium   136 mg
Carbohydrate   33 g
  Dietary Fiber   3 g
  Sugars   25 g
Protein   12 g

2 cups	skim milk
2	medium-size ripe bananas, cut into 1-inch pieces
1/2 cup	plain or banana nonfat yogurt
1/2 cup	nonfat dry skim milk powder
1/3 cup	wheat germ
1 tsp	vanilla
2 1/2 tsp	EQUAL Measure or 8 packets EQUAL sweetener or 1/3 cup EQUAL Spoonful
	Ground cinnamon (optional)

Blend all ingredients except cinnamon in blender or food processor until smooth. Pour into glasses and sprinkle with cinnamon, if desired.

Number of Servings   4

HOLIDAY EGGNOG

SERVING SIZE
4 oz (1/2 cup)

EXCHANGES
PYRAMID SERVINGS
Milk, skim   1

NUTRITION FACTS
Calories   76
Calories from Fat   13
Fat   1 g
  Saturated Fat   1 g
Cholesterol   55 mg
Sodium   79 mg
Carbohydrate   10 g
  Dietary Fiber   0 g
  Sugars   7 g
Protein   6 g

2 cups	skim milk
2 Tbsp	cornstarch
3 1/2 tsp	EQUAL Measure or 12 packets EQUAL sweetener or 1/2 cup EQUAL Spoonful
2	eggs, beaten
2 tsp	vanilla
1/4 tsp	ground cinnamon
2 cups	skim milk, chilled
1/8 tsp	ground nutmeg

1. Mix 2 cups milk, cornstarch, and EQUAL in small saucepan; heat to boiling. Boil 1 minute, stirring constantly. Mix about half of milk mixture into eggs; return egg mixture to remaining milk in saucepan. Cook over low heat until slightly thickened, stirring constantly. Remove from heat; stir in vanilla and cinnamon.
2. Cool to room temperature; refrigerate until chilled. Stir 2 cups chilled milk into custard mixture; serve in small glasses. Sprinkle with nutmeg.

Variation: Stir 1–1 1/2 tsp rum or brandy extract into eggnog, if desired.

Number of Servings   8

RUSSIAN-STYLE TEA

SERVING SIZE
1 cup

EXCHANGES
PYRAMID SERVINGS
Free Food

NUTRITION FACTS
Calories   20
Calories from Fat 0
Fat   0 g
   Saturated Fat   0 g
Cholesterol   0 mg
Sodium   23 mg
Carbohydrate   5 g
   Dietary Fiber   0 g
   Sugars   3 g
Protein   0 g

1 tub	(0.55 oz) sugar-free lemonade-flavored soft drink mix
1 tub	(0.55 oz) sugar-free orange-flavored breakfast beverage crystals
1 cup	unsweetened iced tea mix
10 1/2 tsp	EQUAL Measure or 36 packets EQUAL sweetener or 1 1/2 cups EQUAL Spoonful
1 tsp	ground cinnamon
1/2 tsp	ground cloves
1/2 tsp	ground allspice
	Boiling water

1. Mix dry ingredients together, stirring well. Measure 1 Tbsp mixture (if prepared with EQUAL Measure or packets) or 2 Tbsp mixture (if prepared with EQUAL Spoonful) into each 8-oz mug; fill with boiling water, and stir to blend.
2. Store remaining mixture in covered jar.

Number of Servings   20

COFFEE LATTE

SERVING SIZE
8 oz (1 cup)

EXCHANGES
PYRAMID SERVINGS
Milk, skim   1/2

NUTRITION FACTS
Calories   34
Calories from Fat   1
Fat   0 g
   Saturated Fat   0 g
Cholesterol   1 mg
Sodium   41 mg
Carbohydrate   5 g
   Dietary Fiber   0 g
   Sugars   5 g
Protein   3 g

1 1/4 cups	regular grind espresso or other dark roast coffee
1	cinnamon stick, broken into pieces
6 cups	water
2 1/2 tsp	EQUAL Measure or 8 packets EQUAL sweetener or 1/3 cup EQUAL Spoonful
2 1/2 cups	skim milk
	Ground cinnamon or nutmeg

1. Place espresso and cinnamon stick in filter basket of drip coffee pot; brew coffee with water. Stir EQUAL into coffee; pour into 8 mugs or cups.
2. Heat milk in small saucepan until steaming. Process half of milk in blender at high speed until foamy, about 15 seconds; pour milk into 4 mugs of coffee; spoon foam on top. Repeat with remaining milk and coffee. Sprinkle with cinnamon or nutmeg before serving.

Number of Servings   8

MOCHA SAUCE

SERVING SIZE
1 Tbsp

EXCHANGES
PYRAMID SERVINGS
Free Food

NUTRITION FACTS
Calories   9
Calories from Fat   1
Fat   0 g
   Saturated Fat   0 g
Cholesterol   0 mg
Sodium   8 mg
Carbohydrate   2 g
   Dietary Fiber   0 g
   Sugars   1 g
Protein   1 g

1 cup	skim milk
4 tsp	unsweetened cocoa
2 tsp	cornstarch
1 tsp	instant coffee crystals
1 tsp	vanilla
1 1/4 tsp	EQUAL Measure or 4 packets EQUAL sweetener or 3 Tbsp EQUAL Spoonful

1. Combine milk, cocoa, cornstarch, and coffee crystals in small saucepan. Cook and stir until thickened and bubbly. Cook and stir 2 minutes more. Remove from heat.
1. Stir in vanilla and EQUAL. Cool. Cover and chill.

Makes about 1 cup
Number of Servings   16

FRESH CRANBERRY RELISH

SERVING SIZE
2/3 cup

EXCHANGES
PYRAMID SERVINGS
Fruit   1/2

NUTRITION FACTS
Calories   42
Calories from Fat 2
Fat   0 g
    Saturated Fat   0 g
Cholesterol   0 mg
Sodium   24 mg
Carbohydrate   11 g
    Dietary Fiber   2 g
    Sugars   8 g
Protein   0 g

1	orange
1 pkg	(12 oz) fresh or thawed frozen cranberries
2 medium	tart apples, unpeeled, cored, and coarsely chopped
5 1/4 tsp	EQUAL Measure or 18 packets EQUAL sweetener or 3/4 cup EQUAL Spoonful
1/8 tsp	salt

1. Grate rind from orange and reserve. Peel orange; cut orange into large pieces.
2. Place orange rind, orange pieces, cranberries, and apples in food processor; process until finely chopped. Stir in EQUAL and salt. Refrigerate until ready to serve.

Note: Amount of EQUAL may vary depending on the tartness of the apples and cranberries.

Number of Servings   12

SPICED FRUIT BUTTER

SERVING SIZE
1 Tbsp

EXCHANGES
PYRAMID SERVINGS
Free Food

NUTRITION FACTS
Calories   8
Calories from Fat   0
Fat   0 g
    Saturated Fat   0 g
Cholesterol   0 mg
Sodium   0 mg
Carbohydrate   2 g
    Dietary Fiber   0 g
    Sugars   2 g
Protein   0 g

3 lb	apples, pears, or peaches
3/4 cup	apple juice, pear nectar, or peach nectar
1–2 tsp	ground cinnamon
1/2 tsp	ground nutmeg
1/8 tsp	ground cloves
5 tsp	EQUAL Measure or 16 packets EQUAL sweetener or 2/3 cup EQUAL Spoonful

1. Peel and core or pit fruit; slice. Combine prepared fruit, fruit juice, and spices in Dutch oven. Bring to boiling; cover and simmer until very tender, about 15 minutes. Cool slightly. Purée in batches in blender or food processor. Return to Dutch oven.
2. Simmer, uncovered, over low heat until desired consistency, stirring frequently. (This may take up to 1 hour.) Remove from heat; stir in EQUAL. Transfer to freezer containers or jars, leaving 1/2-inch head-space. Store up to 2 weeks in refrigerator or up to 3 months in freezer.

Makes 6 (1/2-pint) jars
Number of Servings   96

REFRIGERATOR CORN RELISH

SERVING SIZE
2 Tbsp

EXCHANGES
PYRAMID SERVINGS
Starch   1/2

NUTRITION FACTS
Calories   23
Calories from Fat   2
Fat   0 g
  Saturated Fat   0 g
Cholesterol   0 mg
Sodium   62 mg
Carbohydrate   6 g
  Dietary Fiber   1 g
  Sugars   1 g
Protein   1 g

2 cups	cut fresh corn (4 ears) or 1 (10-oz) pkg frozen whole-kernel corn
1/2 cup	vinegar
1/3 cup	cold water
1 Tbsp	cornstarch
1/4 cup	chopped onion
1/4 cup	chopped celery
1/4 cup	chopped green or red bell pepper
2 Tbsp	chopped pimiento
1 tsp	ground turmeric
1/2 tsp	salt
1/2 tsp	dry mustard
1 3/4 tsp	EQUAL Measure or 6 packets EQUAL sweetener or 1/4 cup EQUAL Spoonful

1. Cook corn in boiling water until crisp-tender, 5 to 7 minutes; drain and set aside.
2. Combine vinegar, water, and cornstarch in large saucepan; stir until cornstarch is dissolved. Add corn, onion, celery, pepper, pimiento, turmeric, salt, and mustard.
3. Cook and stir until thickened and bubbly. Cook and stir 2 minutes more. Remove from heat; stir in EQUAL. Cool. Cover and store in refrigerator up to 2 weeks. Serve with beef, pork, or poultry.

Makes 2 1/2 cups
Number of Servings   20

SASSY SWEET AND SOUR DRESSING

SERVING SIZE
2 Tbsp

EXCHANGES
PYRAMID SERVINGS
Free Food

NUTRITION FACTS
Calories   16
Calories from Fat   3
Fat   0 g
    Saturated Fat   0 g
Cholesterol   2 mg
Sodium   111 mg
Carbohydrate   3 g
    Dietary Fiber   0 g
    Sugars   2 g
Protein   1 g

1 cup	plain low-fat yogurt
1/3 cup	cider vinegar
2 Tbsp	finely chopped onion
1 3/4 tsp	EQUAL Measure or 6 packets EQUAL sweetener or 1/4 cup EQUAL Spoonful
1 tsp	dry mustard
1 tsp	celery seed
1/2 tsp	salt

Process all ingredients in food processor or blender until smooth and well mixed. Refrigerate until ready to serve.

Variation: Substitute 1 Tbsp poppy seed for celery seed.

Number of Servings   12

TRIPLE-BERRY JAM

SERVING SIZE
1 Tbsp

EXCHANGES
PYRAMID SERVINGS
Free Food

NUTRITION FACTS
Calories   10
Calories from Fat   1
Fat   0 g
    Saturated Fat   0 g
Cholesterol   0 mg
Sodium   2 mg
Carbohydrate   2 g
    Dietary Fiber   1 g
    Sugars   1 g
Protein   0 g

4 cups	fresh strawberries or thawed frozen unsweetened strawberries
2 cups	fresh raspberries or thawed frozen unsweetened raspberries
1 cup	fresh blueberries or thawed frozen unsweetened blueberries
1 pkg	(1 3/4 oz) no-sugar-needed pectin
2 Tbsp	EQUAL Measure or 20 packets EQUAL sweetener or 3/4 cup plus 4 tsp EQUAL Spoonful

1. Mash strawberries, raspberries, and blueberries, by hand or with food processor, to make 4 cups pulp. Stir in pectin; let mixture stand 10 minutes, stirring frequently. Transfer to large saucepan. Cook and stir over medium heat until mixture comes to a boil. Cook and stir 1 minute more. Remove from heat; stir in EQUAL. Skim off foam, if necessary.
2. Immediately fill containers, leaving 1/2-inch headspace. Seal and let stand at room temperature until firm (several hours). Store up to 2 weeks in refrigerator or 6 months in freezer.

Number of Servings   4 cups or 4 1/2-pt jars

CAPONATA (ITALIAN EGGPLANT DIP)

SERVING SIZE
1/2 cup

EXCHANGES
Starch   1

PYRAMID SERVINGS
Vegetable   3

NUTRITION FACTS
Calories   83
Calories from Fat   17
Fat   2 g
    Saturated Fat   0 g
Cholesterol   0 mg
Sodium   263 mg
Carbohydrate   17 g
    Dietary Fiber   3 g
    Sugars   9 g
Protein   3 g

	Nonstick cooking spray
5 cups	(1 medium) eggplant, diced
1 cup	chopped green pepper
1 cup	chopped onion
1 cup	sliced fresh mushrooms
2 cloves	garlic, minced
1/2 cup	ESTEE Ketchup
1/2 cup	water
1 Tbsp	red wine vinegar
1/2 tsp	each ESTEE Fructose, ESTEE Salt-It, and dried oregano
2 Tbsp	sliced pimento-stuffed olives
1 1/2 Tbsp	pine nuts
	ESTEE Ranch Style Snack Crisps or Italian bread

1. Spray large skillet with nonstick cooking spray; heat over medium heat. Add next 5 ingredients; cook, stirring, 5 minutes. Reduce heat to low, simmer covered about 15 minutes.
2. Add remaining ingredients, and simmer an additional 30 minutes, stirring occasionally. Cool before serving. Serve with ESTEE Ranch Style Snack Crisps or Italian bread. (Bread not included in nutrient analysis.)

Number of Servings   6

LOW-SALT CHILI SAUCE

SERVING SIZE
1/8th recipe

EXCHANGES
Free Food

PYRAMID SERVINGS
Vegetable   1

NUTRITION FACTS
Calories   17
Calories from Fat   1
Fat   0 g
  Saturated Fat   0 g
Cholesterol   0 mg
Sodium   2 mg
Carbohydrate   4 g
  Dietary Fiber   0 g
  Sugars   3 g
Protein   0 g

1	tomato, chopped in small squares
1 Tbsp	wine vinegar
1 Tbsp	honey
1/2	chopped onion
1 tsp	garlic powder

Combine all ingredients in small saucepan. Cook over low heat 1/2 hour.

Number of Servings   8

AMELIA ISLAND PUNCH

SERVING SIZE
1 cup

EXCHANGES
PYRAMID SERVINGS
Fruit   1 1/2

NUTRITION FACTS
Calories   110
Calories from Fat   0
Fat   0 g
   Saturated Fat   0 g
Cholesterol   0 mg
Sodium   0 mg
Carbohydrate   25 g
   Dietary Fiber   0 g
   Sugars   23 g
Protein   1 g

1 tub	CRYSTAL LIGHT Lemonade or Pink Lemonade Flavor Low Calorie Soft Drink Mix
2 cups	cold water
1 can	(46 oz) chilled pineapple juice Crushed ice

1. Place drink mix in punch bowl. Add water; stir to dissolve. Stir in juice.
2. Refrigerate. Serve over crushed ice.

Makes about 2 quarts or 8 (1-cup) servings
Number of Servings   8

FRUITY FRAPPE

SERVING SIZE
1 cup

EXCHANGES
Carbohydrate   1

PYRAMID SERVINGS
Fruit   1/2
Sweet   1/2

NUTRITION FACTS
Calories   80
Calories from Fat   0
Fat   0 g
  Saturated Fat   0 g
Cholesterol   0 mg
Sodium   25 mg
Carbohydrate   18 g
  Dietary Fiber   1 g
  Sugars   13 g
Protein   2 g

3 cups	prepared CRYSTAL LIGHT Fruit Punch Flavor Low Calorie Soft Drink Mix
1 1/2 cups	frozen nonfat vanilla yogurt, softened
1 cup	sliced strawberries
1	ripe banana, cut into chunks

Place prepared drink mix, frozen yogurt, and fruit in blender container; cover. Blend on high speed until smooth. Serve at once.

Makes 6 (1-cup) servings
Number of Servings   6

SHREDDED WHEAT SNACK MIX

SERVING SIZE
1/2 cup

EXCHANGES
PYRAMID SERVINGS
Starch   1
Fat   1/2

NUTRITION FACTS
Calories   100
Calories from Fat   25
Fat   3 g
   Saturated Fat   0.5 g
Cholesterol   0 mg
Sodium   190 mg
Carbohydrate   17 g
   Dietary Fiber   2 g
   Sugars   0 g
Protein   2 g

The party's at your house and you don't want to serve the same old bag of chips and dip. But you don't want to spend a lot of time preparing appetizers either. Here's a snack that's satisfying and so good that folks won't stop eating it till it's all gone!

4 cups	NABISCO Shredded Wheat SPOON SIZE Cereal
1 cup	small unsalted pretzels
1 cup	popped popcorn (not buttered or salted)
3 Tbsp	PARKAY Spread Sticks, melted
1 Tbsp	Worcestershire sauce
1 tsp	seasoned salt

1. Heat oven to 300°F.
2. Mix cereal, pretzels, and popcorn in 15 x 10 x 1-inch baking pan. Mix spread, Worcestershire sauce, and seasoned salt in small bowl. Drizzle evenly over cereal mixture; toss to coat.
3. Bake 30 minutes or until crisp, stirring halfway through baking time.* Cool. Store in tightly covered containers.

Number of Servings   12

*Microwave: Pour mixture into large microwavable bowl. Microwave on HIGH 5 to 6 minutes or until crisp, stirring halfway through cooking time. Continue as above.

Reprinted with permission of Kraft Foods, Inc.

DEB'S DILLY DIP

SERVING SIZE
2 Tbsp

EXCHANGES
Carbohydrate   1/2

PYRAMID SERVINGS
Starch   1/2

NUTRITION FACTS
Calories   45
Calories from Fat   20
Fat   2.5 g
  Saturated Fat   0 g
Cholesterol   0 mg
Sodium   95 mg
Carbohydrate   6 g
  Dietary Fiber   0 g
  Sugars   2 g
Protein   1 g

1 cup	MIRACLE WHIP LIGHT Salad Dressing
1 container	(16 oz) BREAKSTONE'S or KNUDSEN FREE Fat Free Sour Cream
1 Tbsp	dill weed
1 Tbsp	instant minced onion
1 Tbsp	parsley flakes

1. Mix all ingredients. Refrigerate several hours or overnight.
2. Serve with vegetable dippers.

Makes 3 cups
Number of Servings   24

Reprinted with permission of Kraft Foods, Inc.

COOL RASPBERRY FRUIT DIP

SERVING SIZE
2 Tbsp dip

EXCHANGES
Carbohydrate   1/2

PYRAMID SERVINGS
Sweet   1/2

NUTRITION FACTS
Calories   35
Calories from Fat   0
Fat   0 g
  Saturated Fat   0 g
Cholesterol   0 mg
Sodium   170 mg
Carbohydrate   8 g
  Dietary Fiber   0 g
  Sugars   6 g
Protein   0 g

1/2 cup	SEVEN SEAS FREE Raspberry Vinaigrette Fat Free Dressing
1/3 cup	BREYERS Lowfat Vanilla Yogurt
3/4 cup	thawed COOL WHIP LITE Whipped Topping Cut-up fresh fruit

1. Mix dressing, yogurt, and whipped topping until smooth. Refrigerate.
2. Serve with assorted fruits.

Number of Servings   8

Reprinted with permission of Kraft Foods, Inc.

WHITE SANGRIA SPLASH

SERVING SIZE
1/2 cup

EXCHANGES
PYRAMID SERVINGS
Fruit   1

NUTRITION FACTS
Calories   70
Calories from Fat 0
Fat   0 g
  Saturated Fat   0 g
Cholesterol   0 mg
Sodium   55 mg
Carbohydrate   13 g
  Dietary Fiber   2 g
  Sugars   12 g
Protein   2 g

1 cup	dry white wine
2 pkg	(4-serving size) JELL-O Brand Lemon Flavor Sugar Free Low Calorie Gelatin Dessert
3 cups	club soda
1 Tbsp	fresh lime juice
1 Tbsp	orange juice
3 cups	seedless grapes, divided
2 cups	sliced strawberries, divided
4	kiwis, peeled, sliced
	Nonstick cooking spray

1. Bring wine to boil in small saucepan. Stir boiling wine into gelatin in medium bowl 2 minutes or until completely dissolved. Stir in club soda, lime juice, and orange juice. Place bowl of gelatin in larger bowl of ice and water. Let stand about 10 minutes or until thickened, stirring occasionally.
2. Stir in 1 cup of the grapes and strawberries. Pour into 6-cup mold that has been lightly sprayed with nonstick cooking spray.
3. Refrigerate about 4 hours or until firm. Unmold. Garnish with remaining fruit.

Number of Servings   12

Reprinted with permission of Kraft Foods, Inc.

FIESTA NACHOS

SERVING SIZE
1/6th recipe

EXCHANGES
PYRAMID SERVINGS
Starch   3
Fat   1/2

NUTRITION FACTS
Calories   249
Calories from Fat   52
Fat   6 g
   Saturated Fat   2 g
Cholesterol   6 mg
Sodium   636 mg*
Carbohydrate   45 g
   Dietary Fiber   7 g
   Sugars   1 g
Protein   7 g

1 can	(11 oz) CAMPBELL'S condensed Fiesta Nacho Cheese Soup
1/3 cup	water
1 bag	(about 10 oz) tortilla chips, fat free
	Chopped tomato
	Sliced green onions
	Sliced VLASIC or EARLY CALIFORNIA Pitted Ripe Olives
	Chopped green and/or red pepper

1. In small saucepan, mix soup and water. Over low heat, heat through, stirring often.
2. Serve over tortilla chips. Top with tomato, onions, olives, and pepper. If desired, garnish with green onion.

Number of Servings   6

* >400 mg of sodium

Recipe provided courtesy of Campbell Soup Company.

SALSA ONION DIP

SERVING SIZE
2 Tbsp

EXCHANGES
PYRAMID SERVINGS
Saturated Fat   1

NUTRITION FACTS
Calories   48
Calories from Fat   36
Fat   4 g
   Saturated Fat   2 g
Cholesterol   8 mg
Sodium   197 mg
Carbohydrate   3 g
   Dietary Fiber   0 g
   Sugars   2 g
Protein   1 g

1 pouch	CAMPBELL'S Dry Onion Soup and Recipe Mix
1 container	(16 oz) sour cream
1 cup	PACE Thick & Chunky Salsa Assorted fresh vegetables or chips

Mix soup mix, sour cream, and salsa. Refrigerate at least 2 hours. Serve with fresh vegetables or chips for dipping. If desired, garnish with green onion.

Makes 3 cups
Number of Servings   24

Recipe provided courtesy of Campbell Soup Company.

Soups, Salads, and Side Dishes

Creamy Vegetable Medley
Fiesta Rice
Tortellini Salad
Glazed Fruit Salad
Vegetables With Broccoli-Lemon Sauce
Cabbage Slaw
Shredded Carrot and Raisin Salad
Oriental Garden Toss
Penne Salad With Spring Peas
Triple-Bean Salad
Fresh Greens With Hot Bacon Dressing
All-American Barbecued Beans
Pasta Vinaigrette
Sesame Slaw
Fajita Salad
Couscous Salad
Sweet Potatoes a l'Orange
Polynesian Cabbage Slaw
Zucchini Casserole
Savory Brown Rice Pilaf
Cheese Potato Crisps
Southwest Bean & Corn Salad
Gazpacho Salad
Sassy Potato Corn Chowder
Zesty New Potato Salad
Tangy Broccoli Salad
Italian Tuna Salad Toss
LOG CABIN-Glazed Sweet Potatoes
Stuffed Pepper Casserole
Squash Casserole
Fiesta Chicken Soup

Lentil Rice Salad
Herbed Skillet Vegetables
Vegetable Rice Pilaf
Apple Raisin Stuffing
Creamy Potato Soup

CREAMY VEGETABLE MEDLEY

SERVING SIZE
1/2 cup plus

EXCHANGES
PYRAMID SERVINGS
Starch   1/2
Vegetable   1
Fat   1/2

NUTRITION FACTS
Calories   92
Calories from Fat   33
Fat   4 g
   Saturated Fat   2 g
Cholesterol   9 mg
Sodium   493 mg*
Carbohydrate   12 g
   Dietary Fiber   3 g
   Sugars   4 g
Protein   5 g

1 can	(10 3/4 oz) CAMPBELL'S condensed Golden Corn or Cheddar Cheese Soup
1/2 cup	skim milk
2 cups	fresh broccoli florets
2 medium	carrots, sliced (about 1 cup)
1 cup	fresh cauliflower florets
1/3 cup	diced sweet red or green pepper, optional
1/2 cup	shredded Cheddar cheese (2 oz) (optional)
1 Tbsp	chopped fresh cilantro
1/2–1 tsp	Louisiana-style hot sauce (optional)

1. In 2-qt saucepan, combine soup and milk. Over medium heat, heat to boiling, stirring occasionally.
2. Add vegetables. Reduce heat to low. Cover; cook 15 minutes or until vegetables are tender, stirring occasionally.
3. Stir in cheese, cilantro, and hot sauce.
4. Heat until cheese is melted. If desired, garnish with fresh cilantro.

Makes about 3 1/2 cups
Number of Servings   6

* >400 mg of sodium

Recipe provided courtesy of Campbell Soup Company.

FIESTA RICE

SERVING SIZE
1 cup

EXCHANGES
PYRAMID SERVINGS
Starch   2 1/2
Vegetable   2
Fat   1

NUTRITION FACTS
Calories   303
Calories from Fat   76
Fat   8 g
  Saturated Fat   3 g
Cholesterol   12 mg
Sodium   597 mg*
Carbohydrate   47 g
  Dietary Fiber   2 g
  Sugars   7 g
Protein   8 g

1 Tbsp	vegetable oil
1	small green pepper, chopped (about 1/2 cup)
1	small onion, chopped (about 1/4 cup)
3 cups	V8 PICANTE Vegetable Juice
1/4 tsp	garlic powder
1 cup	uncooked regular long-grain rice
1/2 cup	shredded Monterey Jack cheese (2 oz)

1. In 2-qt saucepan over medium heat, in hot oil, cook pepper and onion until tender, stirring often.
2. Add "V8" juice and garlic powder. Heat to boiling. Stir in rice. Reduce heat to low. Cover; cook 15 minutes. Uncover; cook 5 minutes more or until rice is tender and liquid is absorbed, stirring occasionally. Stir in cheese. If desired, garnish with celery leaves.

Makes about 4 cups
Number of Servings   4

* >400 mg of sodium

Recipe provided courtesy of Campbell Soup Company.

TORTELLINI SALAD

SERVING SIZE
1 cup + 2 Tbsp

EXCHANGES
PYRAMID SERVINGS
Starch   1 1/2
Vegetable   1
Fat   1/2

NUTRITION FACTS
Calories   168
Calories from Fat   30
Fat   3 g
   Saturated Fat   1 g
Cholesterol   20 mg
Sodium   339 mg
Carbohydrate   29 g
   Dietary Fiber   1 g
   Sugars   5 g
Protein   6 g

8 oz	frozen cheese-filled tortellini (about 2 cups)
1/2 cup	refrigerated MARIE'S ZESTY Fat Free Italian Vinaigrette
1 small	cucumber, diced (about 1 cup)
1 medium	tomato, diced (about 1 cup)
1	green onion, sliced (about 2 Tbsp)
	Assorted salad greens (optional)

1. Cook tortellini according to package directions. Drain in colander. In medium bowl, toss hot tortellini with vinaigrette; cool 10 minutes.
2. Add cucumber, tomato, and onion; toss gently to coat. Serve at room temperature or cover and refrigerate until serving time. Serve on salad greens. If desired, garnish with plum tomato and fresh sage.

Makes about 4 1/2 cups
Number of Servings   4

Recipe provided courtesy of Campbell Soup Company.

GLAZED FRUIT SALAD

SERVING SIZE
1/5th recipe
(1 cup + about 1 1/2
        Tbsp)

EXCHANGES
Fruit   2 1/2
Fat   1/2

PYRAMID SERVINGS
Fruit   2
Sweet   1/2
Fat   1/2

NUTRITION FACTS
Calories   168
Calories from Fat   24
Fat   3 g
  Saturated Fat   1 g
Cholesterol   0 mg
Sodium   44 mg
Carbohydrate   37 g
  Dietary Fiber   4 g
  Sugars   28 g
Protein   1 g

1 can	(about 11 oz) mandarin orange segments, drained
1 cup	seedless green or red grapes
1 cup	sliced fresh strawberries
2 medium	bananas, sliced
1 medium	apple, cored and diced
1/2 cup	MARIE'S Creamy Glaze for Bananas
1/2 cup	miniature marshmallows (optional)
1/4 cup	flaked coconut, toasted (optional)

1. In large bowl, combine fruit and glaze; toss to coat. Serve immediately, or cover and refrigerate.
2. Just before serving, gently stir in marshmallows and coconut. If desired, garnish with fresh orange mint.

Makes about 5 1/2 cups
Number of Servings   5

Recipe provided courtesy of Campbell Soup Company.

VEGETABLES WITH BROCCOLI-LEMON SAUCE

SERVING SIZE
1/8th recipe

EXCHANGES
PYRAMID SERVINGS
Starch   2
Vegetable   1
Polyunsat Fat   2

NUTRITION FACTS
Calories   267
Calories from Fat   117
Fat   13 g
    Saturated Fat   2 g
Cholesterol   9 mg
Sodium   329 mg
Carbohydrate   34 g
    Dietary Fiber   6 g
    Sugars   4 g
Protein   5 g

3 lb	small red potatoes, quartered
2 cups	fresh broccoli florets
1 large	sweet red pepper, cut into rings
1 can	(10 3/4 oz) CAMPBELL'S condensed Cream of Broccoli Soup
1/2 cup	mayonnaise
4	green onions, finely chopped (about 1/4 cup)
1 Tbsp	lemon juice
1/4 tsp	dried thyme leaves, crushed

1. In 6-qt Dutch oven over high heat, in 1 inch boiling water, cook potatoes 10 minutes.
2. Add broccoli and pepper; cook 5 minutes or until tender. Drain in colander.
3. In 2-qt saucepan over medium heat, combine soup and remaining ingredients. Heat through, stirring occasionally. Pour over vegetables.

Number of Servings   8

Recipe provided courtesy of Campbell Soup Company.

CABBAGE SLAW

SERVING SIZE
1/2 cup

EXCHANGES
PYRAMID SERVINGS
Vegetable   1
Polyunsat Fat   1/2

NUTRITION FACTS
Calories   49
Calories from Fat   35
Fat   4 g
   Saturated Fat   0 g
Cholesterol   0 mg
Sodium   54 mg
Carbohydrate   4 g
   Dietary Fiber   1 g
   Sugars   3 g
Protein   1 g

1 small	head cabbage (1 lb), thinly sliced
1/2 cup	chopped green bell pepper
1/2 cup	chopped onion
2 Tbsp	chopped pimiento or red bell pepper
1/2 cup	cider vinegar
3 Tbsp	vegetable oil
2 1/2 tsp	EQUAL Measure or 8 packets EQUAL sweetener or 1/3 cup EQUAL Spoonful
1 tsp	celery seed
1/2 tsp	dry mustard
1/4 tsp	salt
1/8 tsp	ground black pepper

1. Combine cabbage, green pepper, onion, and pimiento in medium bowl.
2. Measure remaining ingredients into jar; cover with lid and shake to blend well. Pour dressing over cabbage mixture and toss to coat. Refrigerate until ready to serve.

Makes 12 (1/2 cup) servings
Number of Servings   12

SHREDDED CARROT AND RAISIN SALAD

SERVING SIZE
1/6th recipe

EXCHANGES
PYRAMID SERVINGS
Fruit   1
Vegetable   1

NUTRITION FACTS
Calories   82
Calories from Fat   5
Fat   1 g
  Saturated Fat   0 g
Cholesterol   2 mg
Sodium   44 mg
Carbohydrate   18 g
  Dietary Fiber   3 g
  Sugars   15 g
Protein   2 g

1 lb	carrots, peeled and shredded
1 1/2 cups	thinly sliced, cored, peeled apples
1/4 cup	dark raisins
1/2 cup	plain low-fat yogurt or sour cream
1/3 cup	skim milk
1 Tbsp	lemon juice
1/2 tsp	EQUAL Measure or 5 packets EQUAL sweetener or 3 1/2 Tbsp EQUAL Spoonful
1/4 tsp	ground nutmeg
1/4 tsp	ground cinnamon

Combine carrots, apples, and raisins in large bowl. Combine remaining ingredients; spoon over carrot mixture and toss to coat. Refrigerate until chilled.

Number of Servings   6

ORIENTAL GARDEN TOSS

SERVING SIZE
1 cup

EXCHANGES
PYRAMID SERVINGS
Starch   1
Vegetable   1

NUTRITION FACTS
Calories   109
Calories from Fat   19
Fat   2 g
    Saturated Fat   0 g
Cholesterol   0 mg
Sodium   361 mg
Carbohydrate   21 g
    Dietary Fiber   4 g
    Sugars   6 g
Protein   4 g

1/3 cup	thinly sliced green onions
3 Tbsp	reduced-sodium soy sauce
3 Tbsp	water
1 1/2 tsp	roasted sesame oil
1 tsp	EQUAL Measure or 3 packets EQUAL sweetener or 2 Tbsp EQUAL Spoonful
1/4 tsp	garlic powder
1/8 tsp	crushed red pepper flakes
1 pkg	(3 oz) low-fat ramen noodle soup
2 cups	fresh pea pods, halved crosswise
1 cup	fresh bean sprouts
1 cup	sliced fresh mushrooms
1 can	(8 3/4 oz) baby corn, drained and halved crosswise
1	red bell pepper, cut into bite-size strips
3 cups	shredded Chinese cabbage
1/3 cup	chopped lightly salted cashews (optional)

1. Combine green onions, soy sauce, water, sesame oil, EQUAL, garlic powder, and red pepper flakes in screw-top jar; set aside.
2. Break up ramen noodles (discard seasoning packet); combine with pea pods in large bowl. Pour boiling water over mixture to cover. Let stand 1 minute; drain.
3. Combine noodles, pea pods, bean sprouts, mushrooms, baby corn, and bell pepper in large bowl. Shake dressing and add to noodle mixture; toss to coat. Cover and chill 2 to 24 hours. Just before serving, add shredded cabbage; toss to combine. Sprinkle with cashews, if desired.

Number of Servings   6

PENNE SALAD WITH SPRING PEAS

SERVING SIZE
1 cup

EXCHANGES
Starch   3

PYRAMID SERVINGS
Starch   2
Vegetable   1

NUTRITION FACTS
Calories   221
Calories from Fat   7
Fat   1 g
   Saturated Fat   0 g
Cholesterol   1 mg
Sodium   169 mg
Carbohydrate   44 g
   Dietary Fiber   4 g
   Sugars   10 g
Protein   9 g

1 lb	penne or medium pasta shells, cooked and cooled
1 1/2 cups	fresh or thawed frozen peas, cooked
1 large	yellow or red bell pepper, sliced
1/2 cup	sliced green onions and tops
1 cup	skim milk
1/2 cup	fat-free mayonnaise
1/2 cup	red wine vinegar
1/4 cup	minced parsley
2 tsp	drained green peppercorns, crushed (optional)
1 3/4 tsp	EQUAL Measure or 6 packets EQUAL sweetener or 1/4 cup EQUAL Spoonful
	Pepper

1. Combine pasta, peas, bell pepper, and green onions in salad bowl. Blend milk and mayonnaise in medium bowl until smooth. Stir in vinegar, parsley, peppercorns, and EQUAL.
2. Pour dressing over salad and toss to coat; season to taste with pepper.

Number of Servings   6

TRIPLE-BEAN SALAD

SERVING SIZE
1 cup

EXCHANGES
PYRAMID SERVINGS
Starch   1 1/2
Vegetable   1
Monounsat Fat   1/2

NUTRITION FACTS
Calories   159
Calories from Fat 36
Fat   4 g
  Saturated Fat   1 g
Cholesterol   0 mg
Sodium   425 mg*
Carbohydrate   25 g
  Dietary Fiber   7 g
  Sugars   6 g
Protein   8 g

1 can	(14 1/2 oz) green beans, drained
1 can	(14 1/2 oz) wax beans, drained
1 can	(15 1/2 oz) dark kidney beans, drained and rinsed
1/4 cup	sliced green onions
1/4 cup	red wine vinegar
1 Tbsp	olive oil
1 tsp	EQUAL Measure or 3 packets EQUAL sweetener or 2 Tbsp EQUAL Spoonful
1 tsp	dried basil leaves
1 small	clove garlic, minced
1/4 tsp	fresh ground pepper
1/4 tsp	salt (optional)

Combine green beans, wax beans, kidney beans, green onions, vinegar, oil, EQUAL, basil, garlic, and pepper in a large nonmetallic bowl. Mix well. Cover; refrigerate overnight. Serve chilled.

Number of Servings   4

* >400 mg of sodium

FRESH GREENS WITH HOT BACON DRESSING

SERVING SIZE
1 1/3 cups

EXCHANGES
PYRAMID SERVINGS
Vegetable   1
Fat   1/2

NUTRITION FACTS
Calories   61
Calories from Fat   28
Fat   3 g
   Saturated Fat   1 g
Cholesterol   3 mg
Sodium   74 mg
Carbohydrate   7 g
   Dietary Fiber   3 g
   Sugars   4 g
Protein   3 g

3 cups	torn spinach leaves
3 cups	torn romaine lettuce
2 small	tomatoes, cut into wedges
1 cup	sliced mushrooms
1 medium	carrot, shredded
1 slice	bacon, cut into small pieces
3 Tbsp	red wine vinegar
1 Tbsp	water
1/4 tsp	dried tarragon, crushed
1/8 tsp	coarsely ground pepper
1/4 tsp	EQUAL Measure or 1 packet EQUAL sweetener or 2 tsp EQUAL Spoonful

1. Combine spinach, romaine lettuce, tomatoes, mushrooms, and carrot in large bowl; set aside.
2. Cook bacon in 12-inch skillet until crisp. Carefully stir in vinegar, water, tarragon, and pepper. Heat to boiling; remove from heat. Stir in EQUAL.
3. Add spinach mixture to skillet. Toss 30 to 60 seconds or just until greens are wilted. Transfer to serving bowl. Serve immediately.

Number of Servings   5

43

ALL-AMERICAN BARBECUED BEANS

SERVING SIZE
1/2 cup

EXCHANGES
Starch   2
Fat   1/2

PYRAMID SERVINGS
Starch   1 1/2
Sweet   1/2
Fat   1/2

NUTRITION FACTS
Calories   193
Calories from Fat   36
Fat   4 g
    Saturated Fat   1 g
Cholesterol   4 mg
Sodium   552 mg*
Carbohydrate   33 g
    Dietary Fiber   4 g
    Sugars   9 g
Protein   8 g

1 slice	bacon
1/2 cup	chopped onion
1/2 cup	ketchup
2 Tbsp	white vinegar
2 Tbsp	water
1 tsp	prepared mustard
1 tsp	Worcestershire sauce
1/8 tsp	salt (optional)
1/8 tsp	ground black pepper
1 can	(15 1/2 oz) Great Northern beans, drained
2 1/2 tsp	EQUAL Measure or 8 packets EQUAL sweetener or 1/3 cup EQUAL Spoonful

1. Cut bacon into 1-inch pieces; cook in medium saucepan over medium-high heat 3 to 4 minutes. Add onion and cook until bacon is crisp and onion is tender, stirring occasionally.
2. Combine ketchup, vinegar, water, mustard, Worcestershire sauce, salt, and pepper; add to bacon mixture. Stir in beans. Reduce heat and simmer, covered, until flavors are blended, 15 to 20 minutes. Stir in EQUAL.

Microwave Directions
Cut bacon into 1-inch pieces and place in 1 1/2-qt microwavable casserole. Cook uncovered on HIGH 1 minute. Add onion and cook on HIGH 2 1/2 to 3 minutes, stirring once. Combine ketchup, vinegar, water, mustard, Worcestershire sauce, salt, and pepper; add to bacon mixture. Stir in beans and cover with lid or plastic wrap. Cover and cook on HIGH 4 minutes, then cook on MEDIUM 8 to 10 minutes or until flavors are blended, stirring twice. Stir in EQUAL.

Number of Servings   4

* >400 mg of sodium

PASTA VINAIGRETTE

SERVING SIZE
1/6th recipe

EXCHANGES
PYRAMID SERVINGS
Starch   1 1/2

NUTRITION FACTS
Calories   122
Calories from Fat   4
Fat   0 g
   Saturated Fat   0 g
Cholesterol   0 mg
Sodium   86 mg
Carbohydrate   25 g
   Dietary Fiber   1 g
   Sugars   4 g
Protein   4 g

6 oz	pasta (elbows, shells, or fusilli), uncooked
1 cup	shredded carrot
2 Tbsp	Red Wine Vinegar Salad Dressing
1/4 cup	ESTEE Italian Salad Dressing
2 Tbsp	chopped parsley
2 Tbsp	chopped chives

1. Cook pasta as directed on package. Rinse with cold water and drain well. Cool.
2. Combine salad dressings with carrots, parsley, and chives. Add cooled pasta and toss lightly. Chill.
3. Garnish with paprika before serving, if desired.

Number of Servings   6

SESAME SLAW

SERVING SIZE
1/2 cup

EXCHANGES
PYRAMID SERVINGS
Vegetable   1

NUTRITION FACTS
Calories   30
Calories from Fat   12
Fat   1 g
   Saturated Fat   0 g
Cholesterol   1 mg
Sodium   29 mg
Carbohydrate   4 g
   Dietary Fiber   1 g
   Sugars   3 g
Protein   1 g

4 cups	shredded green cabbage
1 cup	shredded carrots
1 cup	thinly sliced radishes
2 cups	alfalfa sprouts, divided
1 Tbsp	toasted sesame seeds
2 Tbsp	reduced-calorie mayonnaise
1/4 cup	plain nonfat yogurt
1 1/2 Tbsp	rice wine vinegar (or apple cider vinegar)
1 tsp	ESTEE Fructose
1 tsp	ESTEE Salt-It
1/4 tsp	celery seed

1. In a large bow,l toss together cabbage, carrots, radishes, 1 cup alfalfa sprouts, and sesame seeds. In a small bowl, whisk together mayonnaise, yogurt, vinegar, fructose, Salt-It, and celery seed; pour over vegetables and toss to coat. Chill before serving.
2. To serve, spread remaining cup of alfalfa sprouts on serving platter, and top with sesame slaw.

Number of Servings   12

FAJITA SALAD

SERVING SIZE
1/4th recipe

EXCHANGES
Starch   1
Vegetable   1
Meat, very lean   3

PYRAMID SERVINGS
Starch   1
Vegetable   1
Meat   1

NUTRITION FACTS
Calories   202
Calories from Fat   32
Fat   4 g
   Saturated Fat   1 g
Cholesterol   48 mg
Sodium   223 mg
Carbohydrate   20 g
   Dietary Fiber   3 g
   Sugars   5 g
Protein   22 g

3/4 lb	lean top round steak, cut into thin strips
2 Tbsp	each: ketchup and lime juice
1 clove	garlic, minced
1/2 tsp	ground cumin
4 cups	shredded lettuce
1/2 cup	each: diced, seeded cucumber, green bell pepper, red bell pepper, and seeded tomato
1/4 cup	each: chopped fresh cilantro* and thinly sliced scallion
1/4 cup	ESTEE Creamy French Dressing
4	6-inch corn tortillas

1. Place beef in a shallow dish. Combine next 4 ingredients; pour over beef, and toss to coat. Refrigerate at least 30 minutes, or overnight, if desired.
2. Meanwhile, arrange lettuce on a large serving platter or shallow salad bowl. In another bowl, combine remaining ingredients, except tortillas, and toss to coat. Spoon over lettuce, leaving a 1-inch border. Salad may be refrigerated if not serving right away.
3. Remove beef from refrigerator. Heat large nonstick skillet over high heat. Add beef and cook, stirring 3 to 5 minutes or just until cooked through; remove from heat. Warm tortillas according to package directions; cut each into thirds. Wrap 2 to 3 pieces of beef in each tortilla strip. Arrange decoratively on top of salad. Serve additional French dressing on side, if desired.

Number of Servings   4

*Fresh cilantro leaves, also called coriander or Chinese parsley, are frequently used in Mexican and Southwestern cooking and can be found in many supermarkets. Do not substitute ground coriander, which comes from the seed of the plant.

COUSCOUS SALAD

SERVING SIZE
1/2 cup

EXCHANGES
PYRAMID SERVINGS
Starch   1

NUTRITION FACTS
Calories   58
Calories from Fat   2
Fat   0 g
  Saturated Fat   0 g
Cholesterol   0 mg
Sodium   56 mg
Carbohydrate   12 g
  Dietary Fiber   1 g
  Sugars   2 g
Protein   2 g

1/2 cup	couscous
1/2 tsp	ESTEE Salt-It
3/4 cup	water
1 cup	diced tomato
2 cups	diced cucumber
1/4 cup	minced red onion
1/4 cup	minced fresh parsley
3 Tbsp	minced fresh mint
1/2 cup	+ 2 Tbsp ESTEE Italian Salad Dressing
2 Tbsp	lemon juice

1. Prepare couscous according to package directions, omitting butter and using ESTEE Salt-lt.
2. In large bowl, combine prepared couscous with remaining ingredients, stirring to blend well. Refrigerate several hours to allow flavors to blend.

Number of Servings   8

SWEET POTATOES A L'ORANGE

SERVING SIZE
1/4th recipe

EXCHANGES
PYRAMID SERVINGS
Starch   1 1/2

NUTRITION FACTS
Calories   112
Calories from Fat   1
Fat   0 g
  Saturated Fat   0 g
Cholesterol   0 mg
Sodium   50 mg
Carbohydrate   26 g
  Dietary Fiber   3 g
  Sugars   13 g
Protein   2 g

2 medium	sweet potatoes or 1 can (17 oz) vacuum-packed whole sweet potatoes (without syrup)
1/2 cup	(1/2 jar) ESTEE Orange Fruit Spread

1. If using fresh sweet potatoes, drop in boiling water to cover. Cook covered approximately 25 minutes. Peel. For canned potatoes, open can and rinse potatoes.
2. Cut potatoes lengthwise, then in 1-inch slices. Arrange in 8 x 8 x 2-inch casserole dish. Spoon orange fruit spread over potatoes.
3. **Microwave:** Cover with plastic wrap. Microwave on MEDIUM/HIGH for 3 minutes or until sauce is melted. Stir. Serve. **Conventional oven:** Cover with foil. Bake at 375°F for 10 to 15 minutes or until sauce is melted. Stir. Serve.

Number of Servings   4

POLYNESIAN CABBAGE SLAW

SERVING SIZE
1/6th recipe

EXCHANGES
PYRAMID SERVINGS
Fruit   1/2
Vegetable   2

NUTRITION FACTS
Calories   81
Calories from Fat   4
Fat   0 g
  Saturated Fat   0 g
Cholesterol   0 mg
Sodium   251 mg
Carbohydrate   19 g
  Dietary Fiber   4 g
  Sugars   13 g
Protein   2 g

1 small	head of cabbage
1 can	(8 1/2 oz) pineapple chunks, packed in juice, drained
1	orange, diced
1/4 cup	green pepper, diced
1/3 cup	ESTEE Thousand Island Salad Dressing
1/3 cup	ESTEE Creamy French Style Salad Dressing
1/3 cup	ketchup

Shred the cabbage and mix in a large bowl with pineapple, orange, and pepper. Combine salad dressing with ketchup and pour over slaw. Mix thoroughly. Chill before serving.

Number of Servings   6

ZUCCHINI CASSEROLE

SERVING SIZE
1/4th recipe

EXCHANGES
Starch   1
Polyunsat Fat   1

PYRAMID SERVINGS
Starch   1/2
Vegetable   1
Fat   1

NUTRITION FACTS
Calories   128
Calories from Fat   68
Fat   8 g
   Saturated Fat   1 g
Cholesterol   0 mg
Sodium   11 mg
Carbohydrate   14

1/8 cup	corn oil
1 lb small	zucchini, sliced
1/8 cup	sliced green onion
3	tomatoes, peeled and sliced (optional)
	Dash pepper
1 clove	garlic, minced
1/2	green pepper, chopped
1/2 cup	grated cheese (optional)
1 1/2 cups	GRAINFIELD's Brown Rice or Crispy Rice, crushed
2 tsp	minced parsley

1. Sauté zucchini and onion in oil, in an oven-proof skillet, until lightly browned. Place tomatoes over zucchini, and sprinkle with pepper, garlic, and green pepper.
2. Cover and bake at 350°F for 20 minutes. Sprinkle with cheese and crushed GRAINFIELD's Brown Rice or Crispy Rice, and bake 20 minutes longer. Sprinkle with parsley just before serving.

Number of Servings   4

SAVORY BROWN RICE PILAF

SERVING SIZE
1/6th recipe

EXCHANGES
PYRAMID SERVINGS
Starch   1
Fat   2

NUTRITION FACTS
Calories   181
Calories from Fat   103
Fat   11 g
  Saturated Fat   2 g
Cholesterol   0 mg
Sodium   12 mg
Carbohydrate   18 g
  Dietary Fiber   1 g
  Sugars   1 g
Protein   2 g

1/2 cup	uncooked long grain rice
6 Tbsp	unsalted mayonnaise, butter, or margarine
1/4 cup	chopped onion
1/2 cup	chopped celery
2 1/2 oz	fresh sliced mushrooms
1/4 cup	sliced water chestnuts
1 cup	GRAINFIELD's Brown Rice
1/4 tsp	ground sage
1/2 tsp	basil leaves
1/8 tsp	pepper
1/2 cup	water

1. Cook rice according to package directions.
2. Melt 2 Tbsp margarine in large skillet. Stir in onion, celery, mushrooms, and water chestnuts. Cook over medium heat, stirring occasionally, about 10 minutes or until celery is almost tender. Add remaining 4 Tbsp margarine; stir until melted.
3. Gently stir in cooked rice, GRAINFIELD's Brown Rice, sage, basil leaves, pepper, and water.

Cover and cook over very low heat about 15 minutes. Serve immediately.

Number of Servings   6

CHEESE POTATO CRISPS

SERVING SIZE
1/6th recipe

EXCHANGES
Starch   1 1/2
Meat, medium fat   1
Saturated Fat   1

PYRAMID SERVINGS
Starch   1 1/2
Meat   1

NUTRITION FACTS
Calories   240
Calories from Fat   102
Fat   11 g
   Saturated Fat   6 g
Cholesterol   29 mg
Sodium   185 mg
Carbohydrate   26 g
   Dietary Fiber   2 g
   Sugars   2 g
Protein   9 g

	Unsalted margarine or butter
5 medium	potatoes, pared
1 1/2 cups	shredded low-salt cheddar cheese
	Paprika
2 cups	GRAINFIELD's Corn Flakes, crushed to measure 1 cup

1. Brush melted butter over bottom of 16 x 11-inch baking pan. Cut potatoes lengthwise into slices about 1/4 inch thick. Arrange slices in single layer in pan, turning once to coat both sides with butter. Sprinkle potatoes with cheese. Top with crushed GRAINFIELD's Corn Flakes. Sprinkle with paprika.
2. Bake 25 minutes at 375°F on a cookie sheet. Excellent served hot or cold.

Number of Servings   6

SOUTHWEST BEAN & CORN SALAD

SERVING SIZE
2 cups

EXCHANGES
PYRAMID SERVINGS
Starch   2 1/2
Vegetable   1

NUTRITION FACTS
Calories   190
Calories from Fat   15
Fat   1.5 g
  Saturated Fat   0 g
Cholesterol   0 mg
Sodium   590 mg*
Carbohydrate   40 g
  Dietary Fiber   5 g
  Sugars   8 g
Protein   8 g

1/2 cup	KRAFT FREE Thousand Island Fat Free Dressing
1/4 tsp	ground black pepper
4 cups	torn mixed salad greens
1 can	(16 oz) black beans, rinsed, drained
1 pkg	(10 oz) frozen corn, thawed, drained
1/2 cup	julienne-cut red pepper
1/2 cup	thinly sliced red onion

1. Mix dressing and black pepper.
2. Arrange greens on serving plate. Top with remaining ingredients. Serve with dressing mixture.

Number of Servings   4

* >400 mg of sodium

Recipe provided courtesy of Campbell Soup Company.

GAZPACHO SALAD

SERVING SIZE
1/6th recipe

EXCHANGES
PYRAMID SERVINGS
Vegetable   1

NUTRITION FACTS
Calories   30
Calories from Fat   0
Fat   0 g
  Saturated Fat   0 g
Cholesterol   0 mg
Sodium   260 mg
Carbohydrate   5 g
  Dietary Fiber   1 g
  Sugars   4 g
Protein   2 g

1 cup	diced tomato
1/2 cup	peeled and diced cucumber
1/4 cup	diced green bell pepper
2 Tbsp	diced red bell pepper
2 Tbsp	thinly sliced green onion
2 Tbsp	vinegar
1/4 tsp	ground black pepper
1/8 tsp	garlic powder
1 1/2 cups	tomato juice
1 pkg	(4-serving size) JELL-O Brand Lemon Flavor Sugar Free Low Calorie Gelatin Dessert Nonstick cooking spray

1. Mix vegetables, vinegar, pepper, and garlic powder in medium bowl. Bring tomato juice to boil in small saucepan. Stir into gelatin in large bowl 2 minutes or until gelatin is completely dissolved. Refrigerate 1 1/4 hours or until slightly thickened (consistency of unbeaten egg whites).
2. Stir in vegetable mixture. Pour into 4-cup mold or bowl that has been sprayed with nonstick cooking spray.
3. Refrigerate 3 hours or until firm. Unmold. Serve with salad greens and garnish with tomato and cucumber slices, if desired.

Number of Servings   6

Reprinted with permission of Kraft Foods, Inc.

55

SASSY POTATO CORN CHOWDER

SERVING SIZE
1/6th recipe

EXCHANGES
Starch   2
Milk, low-fat   1/2
Fat   1

PYRAMID SERVINGS
Starch   2
Milk   1/2

NUTRITION FACTS
Calories   260
Calories from Fat   80
Fat   8 g
    Saturated Fat   2.5 g
Cholesterol   15 mg
Sodium   710 mg*
Carbohydrate   36 g
    Dietary Fiber   3 g
    Sugars   12 g
    Protein   11 g

4 slices	OSCAR MAYER Bacon, chopped
3 cups	cubed peeled potatoes (about 1 1/4 lb)
1 can	(13 1/2 oz) low-sodium chicken broth
1 pkg	(10 oz) frozen corn, thawed, drained
1/2 cup	chopped onion
1/2 cup	sliced celery
2 Tbsp	flour
1/2 cup	MIRACLE WHIP LIGHT Salad Dressing
2 cups	2% milk

1. Cook bacon in large saucepan until crisp; drain. Return to pan.
2. Stir in potatoes, broth, corn, onion, and celery. Bring to boil. Reduce heat to low; simmer 15 minutes or until potatoes are tender.
3. Mix flour and dressing. Stir in milk. Add to potato mixture. Continue cooking 3 to 5 minutes or until thoroughly heated. Sprinkle with additional bacon and parsley, if desired.

Number of Servings   6

* >400 mg of sodium

Reprinted with permission of Kraft Foods, Inc.

ZESTY NEW POTATO SALAD

SERVING SIZE
1/6th recipe

EXCHANGES
PYRAMID SERVINGS
Starch   2

NUTRITION FACTS
Calories   130
Calories from Fat   5
Fat   1 g
   Saturated Fat   0 g
Cholesterol   0 mg
Sodium   200 mg
Carbohydrate   29 g
   Dietary Fiber   2 g
   Sugars   9 g
Protein   2 g

The potato leaps onto the trampoline, splits into quarters and high-jumps into the bowl! If there were an Olympics for potato salads, Zesty New Potato Salad would score a perfect 10. Small red new potatoes team up with Miracle Whip, Dijon mustard, and other on-hand ingredients for a gold medal-winning combination.

1 1/2 lb	new potatoes, quartered (about 4 1/2 cups)
1/2 cup	MIRACLE WHIP FREE Nonfat Salad Dressing
1/4 cup	finely sliced green onions
4 tsp	Dijon mustard
2 tsp	honey
	Dash ground black pepper

1. Cook potatoes in boiling water until tender; drain and rinse with cold water until potatoes are cool.
2. Mix dressing, onions, mustard, honey, and pepper in large bowl.
3. Add potatoes; mix lightly. Refrigerate.

Number of Servings   6

Reprinted with permission of Kraft Foods, Inc.

TANGY BROCCOLI SALAD

SERVING SIZE
1/10th recipe

EXCHANGES
Carbohydrate   1/2
Vegetable   1

PYRAMID SERVINGS
Sweet   1/2
Vegetable   1

NUTRITION FACTS
Calories   90
Calories from Fat   15
Fat   2 g
  Saturated Fat   0 g
Cholesterol   5 mg
Sodium   370 mg
Carbohydrate   14 g
  Dietary Fiber   2 g
  Sugars   10 g
Protein   4 g

1 cup	MIRACLE WHIP FREE Nonfat Salad Dressing
2 Tbsp	sugar
2 Tbsp	vinegar
1 medium	bunch broccoli, cut into florets (about 6 cups)
4 cups	loosely packed torn spinach
1/2 cup	slivered red onion
1/4 cup	OSCAR MAYER Real Bacon Bits
1/4 cup	raisins

1. Mix dressing, sugar, and vinegar in large bowl.
2. Add remaining ingredients; mix lightly. Refrigerate.

Number of Servings   10

Reprinted with permission of Kraft Foods, Inc.

ITALIAN TUNA SALAD TOSS

SERVING SIZE
2 cups

EXCHANGES
PYRAMID SERVINGS
Vegetable   2
Meat, lean   1

NUTRITION FACTS
Calories   100
Calories from Fat   10
Fat   1 g
　Saturated Fat   0 g
Cholesterol   15 mg
Sodium   610 mg*
Carbohydrate   10 g
　Dietary Fiber   1 g
　Sugars   8 g
Protein   12 g

1 pkg	(10 oz) salad greens
1 can	(14 oz) artichoke hearts, drained, quartered
1 can	(9 1/4 oz) tuna in water, drained, flaked
1/2 lb	green beans, cooked, drained
1 cup	sliced plum tomatoes
1 bottle	(8 oz) KRAFT FREE Italian Fat Free Dressing

Place greens on serving platter. Arrange artichokes, tuna, beans, and tomatoes over greens. Top with dressing.

Number of Servings   6

* >400 mg of sodium

Reprinted with permission of Kraft Foods, Inc.

LOG CABIN-GLAZED SWEET POTATOES

SERVING SIZE
1/6th recipe

EXCHANGES
Carbohydrate   3

PYRAMID SERVINGS
Starch   2
Sweet   1

NUTRITION FACTS
Calories   290
Calories from Fat   20
Fat   2.5 g
  Saturated Fat   1.5 g
Cholesterol   5 mg
Sodium   140 mg
Carbohydrate   66 g
  Dietary Fiber   3 g
  Sugars   50 g
Protein   2 g

Sweet memories of Thanksgivings past are recalled as the turkey-day cook covers sweet potatoes with old-fashioned LOG CABIN syrup and butter. Sweet tooths are satisfied when they taste the rich maple flavor. Sweethearts, old and young, love America's favorite "other potato" at Thanksgiving. Glazed Sweet Potatoes—they are oh so sweet.

1/2 cup	LOG CABIN Syrup
1 Tbsp	butter or margarine
1 can	(40 oz) sweet potatoes, drained

1. Bring syrup and butter just to boil in large skillet on medium heat. Reduce heat to low; simmer about 2 minutes.
2. Add sweet potatoes. Cook on low heat 10 minutes, gently turning sweet potatoes frequently to glaze. Garnish with pecan halves, if desired.

Number of Servings   **6**

STUFFED PEPPER CASSEROLE

SERVING SIZE
1/4th recipe

EXCHANGES
Starch   3
Vegetable   1
Meat, medium fat   2
Fat   1

PYRAMID SERVINGS
Starch   3
Vegetable   1
Meat   1
Fat   1/2

NUTRITION FACTS
Calories   469
Calories from Fat   164
Fat   18 g
    Saturated Fat   6 g
Cholesterol   70 mg
Sodium   891 mg*
Carbohydrate   47 g
    Dietary Fiber   7 g
    Sugars   8 g
Protein   27 g

2 1/2 cups	PEPPERIDGE FARM Herb Seasoned Stuffing
1 Tbsp	margarine or butter, melted
1 lb	lean ground beef
1 medium	onion, chopped (about 1/2 cups)
1 can	(14 1/2 oz) whole peeled tomatoes, cut up
1 can	(8 oz) whole kernel corn, drained
2 medium	green and/or red peppers, cut lengthwise into quarters

1. Mix 1/4 cup stuffing and margarine. Set aside.
2. In medium skillet over medium-high heat, cook beef and onion until beef is browned, stirring to separate meat. Pour off fat. Stir in undrained tomatoes and corn. Add remaining stuffing. Mix lightly.
3. Arrange peppers in 2-qt casserole. Spoon beef mixture over peppers.
4. Cover and bake at 400°F for 25 minutes. Sprinkle with reserved stuffing mixture. Bake 5 minutes more or until peppers are tender. If desired, garnish with yellow tomato and fresh chives.

Number of Servings   4

* >400 mg of sodium

Recipe provided courtesy of Campbell Soup Company.

SQUASH CASSEROLE

SERVING SIZE
1/8th serving

EXCHANGES
PYRAMID SERVINGS
Starch   1 1/2
Vegetable   1
Fat   2 1/2

NUTRITION FACTS
Calories   210
Calories from Fat   88
Fat   10 g
  Saturated Fat   4 g
Cholesterol   15 mg
Sodium   618 mg*
Carbohydrate   24 g
  Dietary Fiber   3 g
  Sugars   4 g
Protein   6 g

3 cups	PEPPERIDGE FARM Corn Bread Stuffing
1/4 cup	reduced-calorie margarine, melted
1 can	(10 3/4 oz) CAMPBELL'S condensed Cream of Chicken Soup
1/2 cup	low-fat sour cream
2 small	yellow squash, shredded (about 2 cups)
2 small	zucchini, shredded (about 2 cups)
1/4 cup	shredded carrot
1/2 cup	shredded cheddar cheese (2 oz)

1. Mix stuffing and margarine. Reserve 1/2 cup stuffing mixture. Spoon remaining stuffing mixture into 2-qt shallow baking dish.
2. Mix soup, sour cream, yellow squash, zucchini, carrot, and cheese. Spread over stuffing mixture. Sprinkle reserved stuffing mixture over soup mixture.
3. Bake at 350°F for 40 minutes or until hot. If desired, garnish with fresh oregano and yellow squash.

Number of Servings   8

* >400 mg of sodium

Recipe provided courtesy of Campbell Soup Company.

FIESTA CHICKEN SOUP

SERVING SIZE
1/5th recipe

EXCHANGES
Starch   1 1/2
Meat, very lean   3

PYRAMID SERVINGS
Starch   1 1/2
Meat   1

NUTRITION FACTS
Calories   220
Calories from Fat   24
Fat   3 g
   Saturated Fat   1 g
Cholesterol   55 mg
Sodium   465 mg*
Carbohydrate   24 g
   Dietary Fiber   2 g
   Sugars   3 g
Protein   24 g

	Vegetable cooking spray
1 lb	skinless, boneless chicken breasts, cut into cubes
1 large	green and/or red pepper, coarsely chopped (about 1 cup)
2 tsp	chili powder
1 tsp	garlic powder
2 cans	(14 1/2 oz) SWANSON NATURAL GOODNESS Chicken Broth
1 pkg	(10 oz) frozen whole kernel corn (about 1 3/4 cups)
1 cup	cooked rice, cooked without salt
1 tsp	chopped fresh cilantro or parsley (optional)
5	lime wedges

1. Spray large saucepan with cooking spray and heat over medium heat 1 minute. Add chicken, pepper, chili powder, and garlic powder, and cook 5 minutes, stirring often.
2. Add broth, corn, and rice. Heat to a boil. Reduce heat to low. Cook 10 minutes or until chicken is no longer pink. Stir in cilantro. Serve with lime wedges. If desired, garnish with additional fresh cilantro.

Number of Servings   5

* >400 mg of sodium

Recipe provided courtesy of Campbell Soup Company.

LENTIL RICE SALAD

SERVING SIZE
1/6th recipe

EXCHANGES
PYRAMID SERVINGS
Starch   1 1/2

NUTRITION FACTS
Calories   130
Calories from Fat   9
Fat   1 g
  Saturated Fat   0 g
Cholesterol   1 mg
Sodium   462 mg*
Carbohydrate   25 g
  Dietary Fiber   4 g
  Sugars   4 g
Protein   5 g

1 can	(14 1/2 oz) SWANSON Chicken Broth
1/2 cup	uncooked long-grain rice
1/3 cup	dried lentils
2 Tbsp	chopped fresh parsley
	Generous dash ground red pepper
1 stalk	celery, sliced (about 1/2 cup)
1 medium	red onion, chopped (about 1/2 cup)
1/2 cup	diced green or red pepper
1/2 cup	refrigerated MARIE'S Zesty Fat Free Italian Vinaigrette
	Lettuce leaves

1. In medium saucepan over medium-high heat, heat broth to a boil. Stir in rice and lentils. Reduce heat to low. Cover and cook 20 minutes or until rice is done. Let stand 5 minutes or until liquid is absorbed.
2. In large bowl, toss lentil mixture, parsley, ground red pepper, celery, onion, green pepper, and vinaigrette until evenly coated. Refrigerate at least 2 hours or overnight. Serve on lettuce.

Number of Servings   6

* >400 mg of sodium

Recipe provided courtesy of Campbell Soup Company.

HERBED SKILLET VEGETABLES

SERVING SIZE
1/4th recipe

EXCHANGES
Starch   2

PYRAMID SERVINGS
Starch   2
Vegetable   1

NUTRITION FACTS
Calories   151
Calories from Fat   2
Fat   0 g
    Saturated Fat   0 g
Cholesterol   0 mg
Sodium   311 mg
Carbohydrate   33 g
    Dietary Fiber   5 g
    Sugars   5 g
Protein   5 g

2 Tbsp	cornstarch
1 can	(14 1/2 oz) SWANSON NATURAL GOODNESS Chicken Broth
1/2 tsp	dried thyme leaves, crushed
1/8 tsp	pepper
12 small	new potatoes (about 1 1/4 lb), cut into quarters
2 medium	carrots, cut into 1-inch pieces (about 1 cup)
2 stalks	celery, cut into 2-inch pieces (about 1 1/2 cups)

1. In cup, mix cornstarch and 1/4 broth until smooth. Set aside.
2. In medium skillet, mix remaining broth, thyme, pepper, potatoes, carrots, and celery. Over medium-high heat, heat to a boil. Reduce heat to low. Cover and cook 20 minutes or until vegetables are tender. With slotted spoon, remove vegetables to serving dish.
3. Stir reserved cornstarch mixture and add to liquid in skillet. Cook until mixture boils and thickens, stirring constantly. Serve over vegetables.

Number of Servings   4

Recipe provided courtesy of Campbell Soup Company.

VEGETABLE RICE PILAF

SERVING SIZE
1/4th recipe

EXCHANGES
PYRAMID SERVINGS
Starch   2

NUTRITION FACTS
Calories   140
Calories from Fat   6
Fat   1 g
  Saturated Fat   0 g
Cholesterol   0 mg
Sodium   432 mg*
Carbohydrate   31 g
  Dietary Fiber   1 g
  Sugars   2 g
Protein   3 g

	Vegetable cooking spray
3/4 cup	uncooked long-grain rice
1 can	(14 1/2 oz) SWANSON Vegetable Broth
1/4 tsp	dried basil leaves, crushed
3/4 cup	frozen mixed vegetables without corn, peas, or pasta
1/4 cup	chopped red or green pepper

1. Spray medium saucepan with cooking spray, and heat over medium heat 1 minute. Add rice and cook 30 seconds, stirring constantly. Stir in broth and basil. Heat to a boil. Reduce heat to low. Cover and cook 10 minutes.
2. Stir in vegetables and pepper. Cover and cook 10 minutes more or until rice is done and most of liquid is absorbed. If desired, garnish with fresh chives.

Number of Servings   4

* >400 mg of sodium

Recipe provided courtesy of Campbell Soup Company.

APPLE RAISIN STUFFING

SERVING SIZE
1/8th recipe

EXCHANGES
Starch   2

PYRAMID SERVINGS
Starch   1 1/2
Fruit   1/2

NUTRITION FACTS
Calories   158
Calories from Fat   12
Fat   1 g
    Saturated Fat   0 g
Cholesterol   0 mg
Sodium   569 mg*
Carbohydrate   33 g
    Dietary Fiber   2 g
    Sugars   9 g
Protein   4 g

1 can	(14 1/2 oz) SWANSON NATURAL GOODNESS Chicken Broth
1/4 cup	apple juice
1/2 cup	raisins
1 stalk	celery, sliced (about 1/2 cup)
1 medium	onion, chopped (about 1/2 cup)
5 cups	PEPPERIDGE FARM Cubed Herb Seasoned Stuffing

1. In large saucepan, mix broth, apple juice, raisins, celery, and onion. Over medium-high heat, heat to a boil. Reduce heat to low. Cover and cook 5 minutes or until vegetables are tender. Remove from heat. Add stuffing. Mix lightly.
2. Spoon into 1 1/2-qt casserole. Bake at 350°F for 20 minutes or until hot.

Number of Servings   8

* >400 mg of sodium

Recipe provided courtesy of Campbell Soup Company.

CREAMY POTATO SOUP

SERVING SIZE
1/5th recipe

EXCHANGES
PYRAMID SERVINGS
Starch   1 1/2

NUTRITION FACTS
Calories   103
Calories from Fat   10
Fat   1 g
  Saturated Fat   0 g
Cholesterol   2 mg
Sodium   394 mg
Carbohydrate   20 g
  Dietary Fiber   2 g
  Sugars   5 g
Protein   5 g

1 can	(14 1/2 oz) SWANSON Chicken Broth
1/8 tsp	pepper
4	green onions, sliced (about 1/2 cup)
1 stalk	celery, sliced (about 1/2 cup)
3 medium	potatoes (about 1 lb), peeled and sliced 1/4 inch thick
1 1/2 cups	skim milk

1. In medium saucepan, mix broth, pepper, onions, celery, and potatoes. Over high heat, heat to a boil. Reduce heat to low. Cover and cook 15 minutes or until vegetables are tender. Remove from heat.
2. Put half the broth mixture and 3/4 cup milk in blender or food processor . Cover and blend until smooth. Repeat with remaining broth mixture and remaining milk. Return to pan. Over medium heat, heat through.

Number of Servings   5

Recipe provided courtesy of Campbell Soup Company.

Main Dishes

Sweet and Sour Stir-Fry
Down-Home Barbecued Beef
Grilled Fish With Pineapple-Cilantro Sauce
Chicken and Fruit Salad
Best-Ever Meat Loaf
Macaroni and Cheese
Shortcut Sloppy Joes
Basil Chicken Parmesan
Broccoli Beef Stir-Fry
Baked Onion Chicken
Italian Pepper Steak
Tangy Broiled Chicken
Shrimp Creole
Extra-Easy Lasagna
Easy Chicken Enchiladas
Hot Turkey Sandwiches
Garden Pita Pizzas
Creamy Marinated Baked Chicken
Vegetable and Cheese Pasta
Oriental-Style Sea Scallops
Pasta With Broccoli & Shrimp
Curried Turkey Salad
Chicken Sate
Teriyaki Beef Kabobs
Roasted Rosemary Chicken With New Potatoes and Garlic
Flounder en Papillote
Pork Chops With Apricot Sauce
Baked Stuffed Fish Fillet
Stuffed Boneless Chicken Breasts
Golden Baked Fish
Baked Tuna Supreme

Crispy Baked Chicken
Mexican Meat Loaf
15-Minute Chicken & Rice Dinner
15-Minute Chicken & Stuffing Skillet
Easy Chicken Fettuccine
Quick Chicken Marinara
Breakfast Burrito
Saturday Skillet Breakfast
SHAKE 'N BAKE Chicken Nuggets
Smoked Turkey Crunch Sandwich
Creamy Chicken Broccoli Bake
Creamy Ranch & Parmesan Chicken Salad
Greek Chicken Salad
Ham Sandwich With Nectarine Salsa
Vegetable Turkey Pockets
Chili Corn Pie
Pork Chops With Apple Raisin Stuffing
Lemon-Herb Fish Bake
Beefy Vegetable Skillet
Herbed Crab Cakes
Ham and Asparagus Strata
Szechuan Shrimp
Garlic Pork Kabobs
Oriental Chicken and Vegetable Stir-Fry
Easy Chicken Paprikash
Honey Mustard Chicken
Sweet and Sour Chicken
Chicken Pasta Salad
Quick Chili and Rice
Bean and Rice Burritos
Quick Chicken and Noodles
Smothered Pork Chops
Fish Steaks Dijon
Beef and Pasta
Mexican Beans and Rice

SWEET AND SOUR STIR-FRY

SERVING SIZE
1/4th recipe

EXCHANGES
Starch   1
Vegetable   2
Meat, very lean   3
Fat   1/2

PYRAMID SERVINGS
Starch   1/2
Fruit   1/2
Vegetable   2
Meat   1

NUTRITION FACTS
Calories   276
Calories from Fat   62
Fat   7 g
   Saturated Fat   1 g
Cholesterol   69 mg
Sodium   369 mg
Carbohydrate   26 g
   Dietary Fiber   3 g
   Sugars   15 g
Protein   28 g

1 Tbsp	vegetable oil
1 lb	boneless, skinless chicken breasts, cut into 3-inch strips
1 can	(8 oz) sliced water chestnuts, drained
1 cup	2 x 1/2-inch red bell pepper strips
1/4 cup	chopped onion
2 Tbsp	cornstarch
2 Tbsp	lite soy sauce
1 Tbsp	white vinegar
1 can	(8 oz) pineapple chunks, packed in juice, undrained
1/4 tsp	ground ginger
1/4 tsp	salt (optional)
1 3/4 tsp	EQUAL Measure or 6 packets EQUAL sweetener or 1/4 cup EQUAL Spoonful
1 pkg	(6 oz) frozen pea pods

1. Heat oil in wok or skillet. Add chicken; cook until chicken is no longer pink, 5 to 6 minutes. Remove and set aside. Add water chestnuts, pepper, and onion to wok; cook until vegetables are tender, 3 to 4 minutes, stirring constantly.
2. Combine cornstarch, soy sauce, and vinegar in small bowl; stir to dissolve cornstarch. Add pineapple with juice, ginger, and salt. Add to vegetable mixture; cook until sauce thickens, 2 to 3 minutes, stirring constantly.
3. Stir in EQUAL. Add pea pods and chicken; cook until pea pods and chicken are heated through, 2 to 3 minutes.

Number of Servings   4

DOWN-HOME BARBECUED BEEF

SERVING SIZE
1/4th recipe

EXCHANGES
Carbohydrate   1
Meat, very lean   3
Fat   1

PYRAMID SERVINGS
Vegetable   1
Sweet   1/2
Meat   1

NUTRITION FACTS
Calories   243
Calories from Fat   68
Fat   8 g
　Saturated Fat   3 g
Cholesterol   63 mg
Sodium   550 mg*
Carbohydrate   17 g
　Dietary Fiber   1 g
　Sugars   11 g
Protein   26 g

1 slice	bacon
1/2 cup	chopped onion
1/2 cup	ketchup
1/2 cup	apple juice
1 Tbsp	white vinegar
1 tsp	prepared mustard
1 tsp	Worcestershire sauce
1/8 tsp	salt
1/8 tsp	ground black pepper
2 1/2 tsp	EQUAL Measure or 8 packets EQUAL sweetener or 1/3 cup EQUAL Spoonful
12 oz	thinly sliced roast beef
4	kaiser rolls (optional)

1. Cut bacon into 1-inch pieces; cook in medium saucepan over medium-high heat 3 to 4 minutes or until almost cooked. Add onion; cook 3 to 5 minutes or until bacon is crisp and onion is tender, stirring occasionally.
2. Combine ketchup, apple juice, vinegar, mustard, Worcestershire sauce, salt, and pepper; add to bacon mixture. Reduce heat; cover and simmer until flavors are blended, 15 to 20 minutes.
3. Stir in EQUAL and sliced beef. Serve warm on rolls, if desired.

Microwave Directions
Cut bacon into 1-inch pieces and place in a 1 1/2-qt microwavable casserole. Cook, uncovered, on HIGH 1 minute. Add onion and cook on HIGH for 2 1/2 to 3 minutes or until bacon is crisp and onion is tender, stirring once. Combine ketchup, apple juice, vinegar, mustard, Worcestershire sauce, salt, and pepper; add to bacon mixture. Cook, covered, on HIGH 4 to 5 minutes or until boiling. Cook on MEDIUM 8 to 10 minutes or until flavors are blended, stirring twice. Stir in EQUAL and sliced beef. Serve warm.

Number of Servings   4

* >400 mg of sodium

GRILLED FISH WITH PINEAPPLE-CILANTRO SAUCE

SERVING SIZE
1/6th recipe

EXCHANGES
Fruit   1
Meat, very lean   3
Fat   1/2

PYRAMID SERVINGS
Fruit   1
Meat   1

NUTRITION FACTS
Calories   190
Calories from Fat   26
Fat   3 g
  Saturated Fat   0 g
Cholesterol   36 mg
Sodium   69 mg
Carbohydrate   17 g
  Dietary Fiber   1 g
  Sugars   14 g
Protein   24 g

1 medium	pineapple (about 2 lb), peeled, cored, and cut into scant 1-inch chunks
3/4 cup	unsweetened pineapple juice
2 Tbsp	lime juice
2 cloves	garlic, minced
1/2–1 tsp	minced jalapeño pepper
2 Tbsp	minced cilantro
2 Tbsp	cold water
1 Tbsp	cornstarch
1 to 1 1/2 tsp	EQUAL Measure or 3 to 4 packets EQUAL sweetener or 2 to 3 Tbsp EQUAL Spoonful
	Salt and pepper
6	halibut, haddock, or salmon steaks or fillets (about 4 oz each), grilled

1. Heat pineapple, pineapple juice, lime juice, garlic, and jalapeño pepper to boiling in medium saucepan. Reduce heat and simmer, uncovered, 5 minutes. Stir in cilantro; heat to boiling.
2. Mix cold water and cornstarch; stir into boiling mixture. Boil, stirring constantly, until thickened. Remove from heat; cool 2 to 3 minutes.
3. Stir in EQUAL; season to taste with salt and pepper. Serve warm sauce over fish.

Note: Pineapple-Cilantro Sauce is also excellent served with pork or lamb.

Number of Servings   6

CHICKEN AND FRUIT SALAD

SERVING SIZE
1/4th recipe

EXCHANGES
Fruit   1 1/2
Vegetable   1
Meat, very lean   3

PYRAMID SERVINGS
Fruit   1 1/2
Vegetable   1
Meat   1

NUTRITION FACTS
Calories   222
Calories from Fat   27
Fat   3 g
   Saturated Fat   1 g
Cholesterol   49 mg
Sodium   250 mg
Carbohydrate   28 g
   Dietary Fiber   6 g
   Sugars   20 g
Protein   23 g

1/2 cup	plain nonfat yogurt
1/2–1 tsp	lemon-pepper seasoning
1/2 tsp	dry mustard
1/4 tsp	garlic salt
1/4 tsp	poppy seed
1 1/4 tsp	EQUAL Measure or 4 packets EQUAL sweetener or 3 Tbsp EQUAL Spoonful
1–2 Tbsp	orange juice
4 cups	torn spinach leaves
8 oz	thinly sliced cooked chicken breast
2 cups	sliced strawberries
1 cup	halved seedless green grapes
1 1/2 cups	thinly sliced yellow summer squash
2 medium	oranges, peeled and sectioned
1/2 cup	toasted pecan pieces (optional)

1. Combine yogurt, lemon-pepper seasoning, mustard, garlic salt, poppy seed, and EQUAL in small bowl. Add enough orange juice to reach drizzling consistency; set aside.
2. Line platter with spinach. Arrange chicken, strawberries, grapes, squash, and orange sections over spinach. Drizzle salad with dressing. Sprinkle with pecans, if desired.

Number of Servings   4

BEST-EVER MEAT LOAF

SERVING SIZE
1/8th recipe

EXCHANGES
Starch   1
Meat, medium fat   3
Fat   1/2

PYRAMID SERVINGS
Starch   1
Meat   1
Fat   1/2

NUTRITION FACTS
Calories   319
Calories from Fat   172
Fat   19 g
   Saturated Fat   7 g
Cholesterol   99 mg
Sodium   678 mg*
Carbohydrate   13 g
   Dietary Fiber   1 g
   Sugars   5 g
Protein   23 g

1 can	(10 3/4 oz) CAMPBELL'S condensed Tomato or Cream of Mushroom Soup
2 lb	lean ground beef
1 pouch	CAMPBELL'S Dry Onion Soup and Recipe Mix
1/2 cup	dry bread crumbs
1	egg, beaten
1/4 cup	water

1. In large bowl, mix thoroughly 1/2 cup tomato soup, beef, onion soup mix, bread crumbs, and egg.
2. In 2-qt oblong baking dish, firmly shape meat mixture into 8- x 4-inch loaf.
3. Bake at 350°F for 1 1/4 hours or until meat loaf is no longer pink (160°F internal temperature). Spoon off fat, reserving 1 to 2 Tbsp drippings.
4. In 1-qt saucepan over medium heat, combine remaining tomato soup, water, and reserved drippings. Heat through, stirring occasionally. Serve with meat loaf. If desired, serve with green beans, roasted onions, and cherry tomatoes.

Number of Servings   8

* >400 mg of sodium

Recipe provided courtesy of Campbell Soup Company.

MACARONI AND CHEESE

SERVING SIZE
3/4 cup

EXCHANGES
PYRAMID SERVINGS
Starch   2 1/2
Fat   1

NUTRITION FACTS
Calories   255
Calories from Fat   64
Fat   7 g
  Saturated Fat   3 g
Cholesterol   13 mg
Sodium   744 mg*
Carbohydrate   38 g
  Dietary Fiber   2 g
  Sugars   4 g
Protein   9 g

2 cans	(10 3/4 oz each) CAMPBELL'S condensed Cheddar Cheese Soup
1 soup can	skim milk
2 tsp	prepared mustard
1/4 tsp	pepper
4 cups	hot, cooked corkscrew macaroni (about 3 cups dry)
2 Tbsp	dry bread crumbs
1 Tbsp	margarine or butter, melted

1. In 2-qt casserole, combine soup, milk, mustard, and pepper; stir in macaroni.
2. In cup, combine bread crumbs and margarine. Sprinkle over macaroni mixture.
3. Bake at 400°F for 25 minutes or until hot and bubbling.

Makes about 6 cups
Number of Servings   8

* >400 mg of sodium

Recipe provided courtesy of Campbell Soup Company.

SHORTCUT SLOPPY JOES

SERVING SIZE
1/2 cup + 1 bun

EXCHANGES
Starch   2
Meat, medium fat   2

PYRAMID SERVINGS
Starch   2
Meat   1

NUTRITION FACTS
Calories   312
Calories from Fat   111
Fat   12 g
  Saturated Fat   4 g
Cholesterol   47 mg
Sodium   640 mg*
Carbohydrate   32 g
  Dietary Fiber   2 g
  Sugars   10 g
Protein   18 g

1 lb	lean ground beef
1 can	(11 1/8 oz) CAMPBELL'S condensed Italian Tomato Soup
1/4 cup	water
2 tsp	Worcestershire sauce
1/8 tsp	pepper
6	hamburger buns or Kaiser rolls, split and toasted

1. In 10-inch skillet over medium-high heat, cook beef until browned, stirring to separate meat. Spoon off fat.
2. Stir in soup, water, Worcestershire sauce, and pepper. Reduce heat to low. Heat through, stirring occasionally. Serve on buns.

Makes about 3 cups
Number of Servings   6

* >400 mg of sodium

Recipe provided courtesy of Campbell Soup Company.

BASIL CHICKEN PARMESAN

SERVING SIZE
1 chicken breast half,
1/2 cup rice, sauce

EXCHANGES
Starch   2 1/2
Meat, very lean   3
Fat   1/2

PYRAMID SERVINGS
Starch   2 1/2
Meat   1

NUTRITION FACTS
Calories   340
Calories from Fat   65
Fat   7 g
    Saturated Fat   2 g
Cholesterol   74 mg
Sodium   341 mg
Carbohydrate   35 g
    Dietary Fiber   1 g
    Sugars   6 g
Protein   31 g

2 Tbsp	all-purpose flour
1 1/2 tsp	dried basil leaves, crushed
4	skinless, boneless chicken breast halves (about 1 lb)
1 Tbsp	olive oil
1 can	(10 3/4 oz) CAMPBELL'S HEALTHY REQUEST condensed Tomato Soup
2 Tbsp	Chablis or other dry white wine
2 Tbsp	water
1/4 cup	finely chopped green pepper
2 Tbsp	grated Parmesan cheese
2 cups	hot, cooked rice

1. On waxed paper, combine flour and 1 tsp basil. Lightly coat chicken with flour mixture.

2. In 10-inch skillet over medium-high heat, in hot oil, cook chicken 10 minutes or until browned on both sides. Remove; set aside. Pour off fat.

3. In same skillet, combine soup, wine, water, and remaining 1/2 tsp basil. Heat to boiling. Return chicken to skillet. Reduce heat to low. Cover; cook 5 minutes or until chicken is no longer pink, stirring occasionally. Sprinkle with green pepper and cheese. Serve with rice.

Number of Servings   4

Recipe provided courtesy of Campbell Soup Company.

BROCCOLI BEEF STIR-FRY

SERVING SIZE
3/4 cup stir-fry +
1 cup rice

EXCHANGES
Starch   4
Meat, lean   3

PYRAMID SERVINGS
Starch   3 1/2
Vegetable   1
Meat   1

NUTRITION FACTS
Calories   496
Calories from Fat   126
Fat   14 g
Saturated Fat   3 g
Cholesterol   65 mg
Sodium   786 mg*
Carbohydrate   60 g
Dietary Fiber   3 g
Sugars   9 g
Protein   29 g

1 lb	boneless beef sirloin or top round steak, 3/4 inch thick
2 Tbsp	vegetable oil
2 cups	fresh broccoli florets
1/2 tsp	ground ginger
1/4 tsp	garlic powder or 2 cloves garlic, minced
1 can	(10 3/4 oz) CAMPBELL'S condensed Tomato Soup
2 Tbsp	lite soy sauce
1 Tbsp	vinegar
4 cups	hot, cooked rice

1. Slice beef across the grain into thin strips.
2. In 10-inch skillet or wok over medium-high heat, in 1 Tbsp hot oil, stir-fry half of the beef until browned. Remove; set aside. Repeat with remaining beef.
3. Reduce heat to medium. In same skillet, in remaining 1 Tbsp hot oil, stir-fry broccoli, ginger, and garlic powder until broccoli is tender-crisp.
4. Stir in soup, soy sauce, and vinegar. Heat to boiling. Return beef to skillet. Heat through, stirring occasionally. Serve over rice.

Makes about 3 cups
Number of Servings   4

* >400 mg of sodium

Recipe provided courtesy of Campbell Soup Company.

BAKED ONION CHICKEN

SERVING SIZE
1 breaded chicken
breast half or 2 thighs

EXCHANGES
Starch   1
Meat, very lean   4

PYRAMID SERVINGS
Starch   1
Meat   1

NUTRITION FACTS
Calories   215
Calories from Fat   43
Fat   5 g
  Saturated Fat   1 g
Cholesterol   108 mg
Sodium   628 mg*
Carbohydrate   11 g
  Dietary Fiber   1 g
  Sugars   3 g
Protein   29 g

1 pouch	CAMPBELL'S Dry Onion Soup Mix With Chicken Broth
2/3 cup	dry bread crumbs
1/8 tsp	pepper
1	egg or 2 egg whites
2 Tbsp	water
12	skinless, boneless chicken thighs or 6 skinless, boneless chicken breast halves (about 1 1/2 lb)
2 Tbsp	margarine or butter, melted (optional)

1. With rolling pin, crush soup mix in pouch. On waxed paper, combine soup mix, bread crumbs, and pepper.
2. In shallow dish, beat together egg and water. Dip chicken into egg mixture; coat with crumb mixture.
3. On baking sheet, arrange chicken. Drizzle with margarine. Bake at 400°F for 20 minutes or until chicken is no longer pink.

Number of Servings   6

* >400 mg of sodium

Recipe provided courtesy of Campbell Soup Company.

ITALIAN PEPPER STEAK

SERVING SIZE
1 cup pasta + stir-fry

EXCHANGES
Starch   4
Meat, lean   3
Fat   1/2

PYRAMID SERVINGS
Starch   3 1/2
Vegetable   1
Meat   1

NUTRITION FACTS
Calories   504
Calories from Fat   122
Fat   14 g
  Saturated Fat   3 g
Cholesterol   71 mg
Sodium   569 mg*
Carbohydrate   61 g
  Dietary Fiber   5 g
  Sugars   15 g
Protein   33 g

1 lb	boneless beef sirloin or top round steak, 3/4 inch thick
2 Tbsp	olive or vegetable oil
2 cups	sweet pepper strips (green, red, and/or orange)
1 medium	onion, sliced and separated into rings (about 1/2 cup)
1 tsp	dried oregano leaves, crushed
1/4 tsp	garlic powder or 2 cloves garlic, minced
1/4 tsp	pepper
1 can	(11 1/8 oz) CAMPBELL'S condensed Italian Tomato Soup
1/2 cup	water
4 cups	hot, cooked fusilli or spaghetti

1. Slice beef across the grain into thin strips. In 10-inch skillet over medium-high heat, in 1 Tbsp hot oil, cook half of the beef until browned, stirring often. Remove; set aside. Repeat with remaining beef.
2. Reduce heat to medium. In same skillet, in remaining 1 Tbsp hot oil, cook sweet peppers, onion, oregano, garlic powder, and pepper until vegetables are tender, stirring often.
3. Stir in soup and water. Heat to boiling. Return beef to skillet. Heat through, stirring occasionally. Serve over fusilli. If desired, serve with garlic bread.

Number of Servings   4

* >400 mg of sodium

Recipe provided courtesy of Campbell Soup Company.

TANGY BROILED CHICKEN

SERVING SIZE
1 breast half

EXCHANGES
Carbohydrate   1/2
Meat, very lean   3

PYRAMID SERVINGS
Sweet   1/2
Meat   1

NUTRITION FACTS
Calories   166
Calories from Fat   26
Fat   3 g
  Saturated Fat   1 g
Cholesterol   69 mg
Sodium   281 mg
Carbohydrate   8 g
  Dietary Fiber   0 g
  Sugars   5 g
Protein   25 g

6	skinless, boneless chicken breast halves (about 1 1/2 lb)
1 cup	refrigerated MARIE'S ZESTY Fat Free Red Wine Vinaigrette
3/4 cup	LIGHT 'N TANGY V8 Vegetable Juice or V8 PICANTE Vegetable Juice
1 Tbsp	cornstarch

1. Place large plastic bag in deep bowl; add chicken. In 2-cup measure, combine vinaigrette and "V8" juice; pour over chicken. Close bag.
2. Refrigerate at least 4 hours or overnight, turning chicken occasionally. Remove chicken from marinade and arrange on rack in broiler pan. Reserve marinade.
3. In 1-qt saucepan, stir together cornstarch and reserved marinade until smooth. Over medium heat, cook until sauce boils and thickens, stirring constantly.
4. Brush chicken with sauce. Broil 4 inches from heat 15 minutes or until chicken is no longer pink, turning once and brushing often with sauce during cooking. If desired, serve with orange-onion salad and parslied noodles.

Number of Servings   6

Recipe provided courtesy of Campbell Soup Company.

SHRIMP CREOLE

SERVING SIZE
1 cup

EXCHANGES
Starch   4
Meat, very lean   2

PYRAMID SERVINGS
Starch   3 1/2
Vegetable   1
Meat   1

NUTRITION FACTS
Calories   391
Calories from Fat   64
Fat   7 g
  Saturated Fat   1 g
Cholesterol   161 mg
Sodium   607 mg*
Carbohydrate   57 g
  Dietary Fiber   2 g
  Sugars   6 g
Protein   23 g

2 Tbsp	margarine or butter
1 large	green pepper, diced (about 1 cup)
2 ribs	celery, thinly sliced (about 1 cup)
1 medium	onion, chopped (about 1/2 cup)
1/2 tsp	dried oregano leaves, crushed
1/4 tsp	garlic powder or 2 cloves garlic, minced
1/8 tsp	ground red pepper (cayenne)
1 1/2 cups	CAMPBELL'S Tomato Juice
1 Tbsp	cornstarch
16	large shrimp, shelled and deveined
4 cups	hot, cooked parslied rice

1. In 10-inch skillet over medium heat, in hot margarine, cook green pepper, celery, onion, oregano, garlic powder, and red pepper until vegetables are tender-crisp, stirring often.
2. Add 1 cup tomato juice. Heat to boiling. Reduce heat to low. Cover; cook 5 minutes, stirring occasionally.
3. Meanwhile, in small bowl, stir together cornstarch and remaining 1/2 cup tomato juice until smooth.
4. Increase heat to medium. Add cornstarch mixture and shrimp to vegetable mixture. Cook until mixture boils and thickens and shrimp turn pink and opaque, stirring constantly. Serve over rice.

Makes about 4 cups
Number of Servings   4

* >400 mg of sodium

Recipe provided courtesy of Campbell Soup Company.

EXTRA-EASY LASAGNA

SERVING SIZE
1/8th recipe

EXCHANGES
Starch   2 1/2
Meat, medium fat   2
Saturated Fat   1

PYRAMID SERVINGS
Starch   2 1/2
Meat   1
Fat   1

NUTRITION FACTS
Calories   408
Calories from Fat   161
Fat   18 g
   Saturated Fat   9 g
Cholesterol   62 mg
Sodium   678 mg*
Carbohydrate   36 g
   Dietary Fiber   2 g
   Sugars   13 g
Protein   25 g

3/4 lb	lean ground beef
3 cups	PREGO Traditional Spaghetti Sauce
1 container	(15 oz) ricotta cheese
2 cups	shredded mozzarella cheese (8 oz)
6	uncooked lasagna noodles
1/4 cup	water

1. In 10-inch skillet over medium-high heat, cook beef until browned, stirring to separate meat. Spoon off fat. Add spaghetti sauce; heat through, stirring occasionally.
2. In 2-qt oblong baking dish, spread 1 1/2 cups meat mixture. Top with 3 uncooked lasagna noodles, half of the ricotta cheese and half of the mozzarella cheese. Repeat layers. Top with remaining meat mixture.
3. Slowly pour water around inside edges of baking dish. Cover tightly with foil.
4. Bake at 375°F for 45 minutes. Uncover; bake 10 minutes more. Let stand 10 minutes before serving.

Number of Servings   8

* >400 mg of sodium

Recipe provided courtesy of Campbell Soup Company.

EASY CHICKEN ENCHILADAS

SERVING SIZE
1/4th recipe

EXCHANGES
Starch   2
Meat, medium fat   3

PYRAMID SERVINGS
Starch   2
Meat   1

NUTRITION FACTS
Calories   398
Calories from Fat   164
Fat   18 g
    Saturated Fat   10 g
Cholesterol   82 mg
Sodium   978 mg*
Carbohydrate   31 g
    Dietary Fiber   4 g
    Sugars   2 g
Protein   30 g

1 can	(10 oz) enchilada sauce
2 cans	(5 oz each) SWANSON Premium Chunk White Chicken, drained
1 1/2 cups	shredded cheddar cheese
1 can	(4 oz) chopped green chilies
1 small	onion, chopped (about 1/4 cup)
8	corn tortillas (6 inches each)

1. Spread 1/2 can enchilada sauce in 3-qt oblong baking dish; set aside.
2. Combine chicken, 1 cup cheese, chilies, and onion. Along one side of each tortilla, spread about 1/3 cup of mixture; roll up, jelly-roll fashion. Place seam-side down in dish.
3. Pour remaining 1/2 can enchilada sauce over enchiladas. Sprinkle with remaining 1/2 cup cheese. Cover with foil; bake at 350°F for 2 minutes or until hot. If desired, top with shredded lettuce, sour cream, and diced tomato.

Number of Servings   4

* >400 mg of sodium

Recipe provided courtesy of Campbell Soup Company.

HOT TURKEY SANDWICHES

SERVING SIZE
1/4th recipe

EXCHANGES
Starch   1 1/2
Meat, medium fat   2

PYRAMID SERVINGS
Starch   1 1/2
Meat   1

NUTRITION FACTS
Calories   266
Calories from Fat   97
Fat   11 g
  Saturated Fat   3 g
Cholesterol   45 mg
Sodium   624 mg*
Carbohydrate   21 g
  Dietary Fiber   2 g
  Sugars   3 g
Protein   20 g

2 Tbsp	margarine or butter
2 small	carrots, thinly sliced diagonally (about 1/2 cup)
1 medium	onion, chopped (about 1/2 cup)
1/4 cup	sliced celery
3/4 tsp	chopped fresh thyme leaves or 1/4 tsp dried thyme leaves, crushed
1 can	(10 1/2 oz) FRANCO-AMERICAN Turkey Gravy
1/2 lb	sliced cooked turkey
4 pieces	diagonally sliced Italian bread

1. In 2-qt saucepan over medium heat, in hot margarine, cook carrots, onion, celery, and thyme until tender, stirring occasionally.
2. Stir in gravy. Heat to boiling. Add turkey. Heat through, stirring occasionally. Divide turkey and gravy mixture evenly among bread slices. If desired, serve with apples and grapes; garnish with fresh thyme.

Number of Servings   4

* >400 mg of sodium

Recipe provided courtesy of Campbell Soup Company.

GARDEN PITA PIZZAS

SERVING SIZE
1 "pizza"

EXCHANGES
Starch   1
Vegetable   1
Meat, medium fat   1

PYRAMID SERVINGS
Starch   1
Vegetable   1
Meat   1/2

NUTRITION FACTS
Calories   180
Calories from Fat   61
Fat   7 g
   Saturated Fat   3 g
Cholesterol   11 mg
Sodium   478 mg*
Carbohydrate   23 g
   Dietary Fiber   3 g
   Sugars   6 g
Protein   9 g

3	whole wheat pita breads (6-inch rounds)
1 Tbsp	olive or vegetable oil
1 1/2 cups	fresh broccoli florets
3 medium	carrots, thinly sliced (about 1 cup)
1 large	green pepper, chopped (about 1 cup)
1	green onion, chopped (about 2 Tbsp)
1 cup	pizza sauce with sliced mushrooms
1 cup	shredded mozzarella cheese (4 oz)

1. Split each pita bread into two flat rounds, making 6 rounds. Place on 2 baking sheets.
2. Bake at 400°F for 5 minutes or until toasted.
3. In 10-inch skillet over medium heat, in hot oil, stir-fry vegetables until tender-crisp, stirring often. Set aside.
4. Spread each round with 2 rounded Tbsp pizza sauce; top with vegetables and cheese. Bake 5 minutes or until cheese melts.

Number of Servings   6

* >400 mg of sodium

Recipe provided courtesy of Campbell Soup Company.

CREAMY MARINATED BAKED CHICKEN

SERVING SIZE
1 breast half

EXCHANGES
Starch   1
Meat, very lean   4

PYRAMID SERVINGS
Starch   1
Meat   1 1/2

NUTRITION FACTS
Calories   233
Calories from Fat   40
Fat   4 g
   Saturated Fat   1 g
Cholesterol   86 mg
Sodium   410 mg*
Carbohydrate   11 g
   Dietary Fiber   1 g
   Sugars   1 g
Protein   35 g

4 whole	boneless, skinless chicken breasts (about 2 1/2 lb)
1 cup	GUILT FREE Nonfat Cottage Cheese
1 small	onion, coarsely chopped (about 4 oz)
2 Tbsp	lemon juice
2 Tbsp	Dijon mustard
1 tsp	salt-free lemon-pepper seasoning
1/2 tsp	dried oregano
	Nonstick cooking spray
1 cup	dry bread crumbs
1 tsp	salt

1. Split breasts; remove any fat. Place meat into shallow pan or dish.
2. Blend cottage cheese, onion, lemon juice, mustard, lemon-pepper, seasoning, and oregano until smooth.
3. Pour mixture over all sides of chicken. Cover dish; refrigerate at least 8 hours.
4. Heat oven to 400°F. Spray baking pan lightly with vegetable oil.
5. Combine bread crumbs and salt in shallow dish; stir. Dredge each chicken breast into bread crumbs, coating both sides.
6. Arrange chicken in baking pan. Bake until golden, about 25 minutes.

Number of Servings   8

* >400 mg of sodium

VEGETABLE AND CHEESE PASTA

SERVING SIZE
1/4th recipe

EXCHANGES
PYRAMID SERVINGS
Starch   4 1/2
Vegetable   1
Meat, very lean   1

NUTRITION FACTS
Calories   427
Calories from Fat   49
Fat   5 g
   Saturated Fat   2 g
Cholesterol   87 mg
Sodium   579 mg*
Carbohydrate   70 g
   Dietary Fiber   5 g
   Sugars   8 g
Protein   24 g

1 can	(14 1/2 oz) vegetable broth
1 pkg	(1 lb) BIRD'S EYE frozen broccoli, cauliflower & carrots
1 cup	GUILT FREE Nonfat Cottage Cheese
1/4 cup	grated Romano cheese
2 Tbsp	chopped fresh basil leaves
1/4 tsp	crushed red pepper
	Salt and pepper to taste
12 oz	dried fettuccine pasta

1. Bring broth to boil in medium saucepan. Add frozen vegetables; cover and cook over medium heat until vegetables are tender. Drain vegetables over bowl to catch broth. Return vegetables to saucepan; set pan aside.
2. Blend cottage cheese with 1/2 cup of the broth until smooth. Add purée to vegetables in saucepan. Stir in grated cheese, basil, and red pepper. Season to taste with salt and pepper. Warm mixture over low heat while pasta is cooking.
3. Cook pasta according to package directions; drain. Transfer hot pasta to large bowl. Add warm vegetable-cheese mixture. Combine thoroughly. Serve immediately.

Number of Servings   4

* >400 mg of sodium

ORIENTAL-STYLE SEA SCALLOPS

SERVING SIZE
1/6th recipe

EXCHANGES
Starch   2 1/2
Vegetable   2
Meat, lean 1

PYRAMID SERVINGS
Starch   2 1/2
Vegetable   2
Meat, lean 1/1

NUTRITION FACTS
Calories   316
Calories from Fat   54
Fat   6 g
  Saturated Fat   1 g
Cholesterol   25 mg
Sodium   425 mg*
Carbohydrate   47 g
  Dietary Fiber   5 g
  Sugars   8 g
Protein   20 g

* >400 mg of sodium
†Or substitute 2 tsp five-spice powder for star anise and coriander; amounts of vinegar and soy sauce may need to be adjusted to taste.

2 Tbsp	sesame or vegetable oil
1 1/2 cups	broccoli florets
1 cup	thinly sliced onion
1 lb	sea scallops
3 cups	thinly sliced napa cabbage or bok choy
2 cups	snow peas, ends trimmed
1 cup	shiitake or button mushrooms, sliced
2 cloves	garlic, minced
2 tsp	ground star aniset
1/4 tsp	ground coriander†
1/2 cup	low-sodium chicken broth
1/4 cup	rice wine vinegar
2 to 3 Tbsp	reduced-sodium soy sauce
1/4 cup	cold water
2 Tbsp	cornstarch
1 to 1 1/2 tsp	EQUAL Measure or 3 to 4 packets EQUAL sweetener or 2 to 3 Tbsp EQUAL Spoonful
4 cups	hot, cooked rice

1. Heat oil in wok or large skillet. Stir-fry broccoli and onion 3 to 4 minutes. Add scallops, cabbage, snow peas, mushrooms, garlic, anise, and coriander; stir-fry 2 to 3 minutes.

2. Add chicken broth, vinegar, and soy sauce; heat to boiling. Reduce heat and simmer, uncovered, until scallops are cooked and vegetables are tender, about 5 minutes. Heat to boiling.

3. Mix cold water and cornstarch. Stir cornstarch mixture into boiling mixture; boil, stirring constantly with a wire whisk, until thickened. Remove from heat; let stand 2 to 3 minutes. Stir in EQUAL. Serve over rice.

Number of Servings   6

PASTA WITH BROCCOLI & SHRIMP

SERVING SIZE
1 1/2 cups

EXCHANGES
Starch   1
Vegetable   1
Meat, very lean   2

PYRAMID SERVINGS
Starch   1
Vegetable   1
Meat   1

NUTRITION FACTS
Calories   186
Calories from Fat   17
Fat   2 g
   Saturated Fat   0 g
Cholesterol   119 mg
Sodium   245 mg
Carbohydrate   24 g
   Dietary Fiber   4 g
   Sugars   6 g
   Protein   18 g

1/4 lb	Rotelle pasta
1 1/2 tsp	ESTEE Salt-It, divided
1 Tbsp + 1 tsp	lemon juice, divided
1 lb	fresh broccoli, trimmed, cut into bite-sized pieces (4 cups) or 4 cups frozen broccoli florets from a 16- to 20-oz bag
3/4 lb	large fresh shrimp, peeled and deveined or 1/2 lb pre-peeled and deveined frozen shrimp
1/2 cup	chopped onion
1/2 cup	ESTEE Creamy Italian Salad Dressing
1/3 cup	chopped fresh dill or 1/2 Tbsp dried dill
1/2 tsp	ESTEE Fructose Black pepper (to taste)

1. Cook pasta according to package directions, using 1 tsp Salt-It instead of salt; drain and place in large bowl. In large saucepan, bring 4 inches water and 1 Tbsp lemon juice to a boil.
2. Add broccoli and shrimp and cook just until shrimp turn pink and broccoli is fork tender; drain and add to pasta. Add onion and toss.
3. In small bowl, stir together salad dressing, dill, fructose, remaining lemon juice, and Salt-It; add black pepper to taste. Pour over pasta mixture and toss to coat. Serve warm or cold.

Number of Servings   4

CURRIED TURKEY SALAD

SERVING SIZE
1 cup

EXCHANGES
Carbohydrate   1/2
Vegetable   1
Meat, very lean   3
Polyunsat Fat   1/2

PYRAMID SERVINGS
Fruit   1/2
Vegetable   1
Meat   1

NUTRITION FACTS
Calories   185
Calories from Fat   49
Fat   5 g
  Saturated Fat   1 g
Cholesterol   62 mg
Sodium   170 mg
Carbohydrate   12 g
  Dietary Fiber   2 g
  Sugars   8 g
Protein   22 g

1 can	(10 1/2 oz) low-sodium chicken broth
3/4 lb	turkey breast cutlets
1 cup	diced, unpeeled apples
1 cup	thinly sliced celery
1 cup	diced green pepper
1/4 cup	chopped red onion
1/4 cup	reduced-calorie mayonnaise
2 Tbsp	ESTEE Peach Fruit Spread
2 tsp	curry powder
2 tsp	ESTEE Fructose
1/2 tsp	ESTEE Salt-It
	Shredded lettuce for garnish
1/4 cup	diced, dried apricot halves (optional)

1. In a large skillet, bring chicken broth to a simmer over low heat. Add cutlets; cover and cook 3 to 5 minutes or until cooked through.
2. Remove cutlets set aside to cool. Reserve 3 Tbsp broth. When cutlets are cool enough to handle, dice.
3. Place in large bowl with apples, celery, green pepper, and onions; toss.
4. In small bowl, blend reserved broth and next 5 ingredients. Pour over turkey mixture and toss to coat.
5. Chill before serving. Serve on lettuce. Sprinkle with apricots, if desired.

Number of Servings   4

CHICKEN SATE

SERVING SIZE
1/4th recipe

EXCHANGES
Carbohydrate   1/2
Meat, very lean   3
Fat   1/2

PYRAMID SERVINGS
Sweet   1/2
Meat   1

NUTRITION FACTS
Calories   181
Calories from Fat   55
Fat   6 g
   Saturated Fat   1 g
Cholesterol   52 mg
Sodium   395 mg
Carbohydrate   10 g
   Dietary Fiber   1 g
   Sugars   8 g
Protein   21 g

8	wooden skewers
3/4 lb	skinless, boneless chicken breasts

MARINADE

1/4 cup	ESTEE Lite Syrup Maple
2 Tbsp	ketchup
1 Tbsp	lite soy sauce
1 clove	garlic, minced
1 tsp	curry powder

PEANUT SAUCE

2 Tbsp	each: balsamic vinegar
2 Tbsp	low-sodium chicken broth
2 Tbsp	ESTEE Peanut Butter
1 Tbsp	ESTEE Fructose
1 Tbsp	low-sodium soy sauce
1 clove	garlic, minced
1/4 cup	sliced scallions, divided
	Nonstick cooking spray

1. Soak skewers in water while preparing chicken and sauce. Cut chicken into 16 strips, and place in shallow dish. Combine ingredients for marinade; pour over chicken and toss to coat. Refrigerate 1 hour.
2. Meanwhile, in blender or food processor, combine all ingredients for peanut sauce, using half the scallions. Blend until smooth. Pour into small serving dish, and sprinkle with remaining scallions. Remove skewers from water. Thread 2 strips of chicken on each skewer.
3. Heat oven to broil or highest setting. Spray broiler rack with nonstick cooking spray. Place skewers on rack, and broil 7 to 8 minutes, turning once, until chicken is cooked through. Serve with peanut sauce.

Number of Servings   4

TERIYAKI BEEF KABOBS

SERVING SIZE
2 kabobs

EXCHANGES
Vegetable   2
Meat, lean   3

PYRAMID SERVINGS
Vegetable   2
Meat   1

NUTRITION FACTS
Calories   195
Calories from Fat   59
Fat   7 g
   Saturated Fat   2 g
Cholesterol   59 mg
Sodium   210 mg
Carbohydrate   13 g
   Dietary Fiber   2 g
   Sugars   9 g
Protein   22 g

MARINADE

3 Tbsp	ESTEE Breakfast Syrup
1 1/2 Tbsp	ketchup
1 1/2 Tbsp	reduced-sodium soy sauce
2 cloves	garlic, minced
1 tsp	minced fresh ginger

KABOBS

1 lb	lean top round beef steak
8	wooden skewers
1 large	onion, cut into 8 wedges
1	green bell pepper, cut into 8 pieces
8	cherry tomatoes

1. Cut beef lengthwise into 16 thin, strips. Set aside. Combine marinade ingredients in a shallow dish. Add beef, toss to coat. Refrigerate at least 30 minutes or overnight.
2. Heat oven to broil. Remove beef from marinade and thread onto skewers alternately with onion and pepper. Add tomato to the end of each skewer.
3. Spray broiling rack with nonstick cooking spray. Add kabobs and broil 3 to 4 inches from heat source, 2 to 3 minutes on each side.

Number of Servings   4

ROASTED ROSEMARY CHICKEN WITH NEW POTATOES AND GARLIC

SERVING SIZE
1/4th recipe

EXCHANGES
Starch   1 1/2
Meat, very lean   4

PYRAMID SERVINGS
Starch   1 1/2
Meat   1 1/2

NUTRITION FACTS
Calories   255
Calories from Fat   48
Fat   5 g
    Saturated Fat   1 g
Cholesterol   69 mg
Sodium   110 mg
Carbohydrate   23 g
    Dietary Fiber   3 g
    Sugars   7 g
Protein   28 g

	Nonstick cooking spray
4 Tbsp	ESTEE Italian Dressing, divided
	Juice of 1/2 lemon
4	boneless, skinless chicken breasts, trimmed of fat (about 1 lb)
2 tsp	olive oil
4	new potatoes, quartered (about 3/4 lb)
1	onion, cut into 8 wedges
1 tsp	dried rosemary, crushed
1/4 tsp	ESTEE Salt-It
	Black pepper
1/4 cup	white wine
2 cloves	garlic, minced

1. Preheat oven to 450°F. Line roasting pan with aluminum foil; spray with nonstick cooking spray.
2. In shallow dish, combine half the salad dressing with lemon juice. Add chicken and toss to coat. Place each breast in center of roasting pan.
3. Combine remaining salad dressing and oil in bowl; add potatoes and onion and toss to coat. Scatter around chicken. Sprinkle seasonings over chicken and vegetables. Bake 15 minutes. Add wine to roasting pan. Bake 20 more minutes, basting occasionally. Add garlic during the last 5 minutes of cooking.

Number of Servings   4

FLOUNDER EN PAPILLOTE

SERVING SIZE
1/4 recipe (1 fillet + vegetables)

EXCHANGES
Vegetable   1
Meat, very lean   3

PYRAMID SERVINGS
Vegetable   1
Meat   1

NUTRITION FACTS
Calories   123
Calories from Fat   15
Fat   2 g
  Saturated Fat   0 g
Cholesterol   60 mg
Sodium   136 mg
Carbohydrate   4 g
  Dietary Fiber   1 g
  Sugars   2 g
Protein   22 g

	Nonstick cooking spray
1/2 cup	julienned red bell pepper
1/2 cup	zucchini
1/2 cup	leeks
1/2 tsp	ESTEE Seasoned Salt-It, divided
1/4 cup	ESTEE Creamy Italian Salad Dressing
1 Tbsp	minced fresh parsley
1 tsp	lemon juice
	Parchment paper or aluminum foil
	Black pepper
4	4-oz flounder fillets

1. Preheat oven to 400°F. Spray large skillet with nonstick cooking spray; heat over medium heat. Add vegetables; cook, stirring occasionally, 3 to 5 minutes or until crisp-tender. Remove from heat; add 1/4 tsp ESTEE Seasoned Salt-It.
2. In small bowl, stir together dressing, parsley, and lemon juice. Cut four 15 x 12-inch pieces of parchment paper or aluminum foil; fold in half lengthwise. Trim each into a large heart shape; place on baking sheet.
3. Spoon vegetables evenly over half of each parchment heart near the crease. Spoon half of dressing mixture over vegetables. Season flounder fillets with remaining ESTEE Seasoned Salt-It and black pepper to taste. Top with fillets; spoon on remaining dressing mixture.
4. Starting with rounded edge of each heart, pleat and crimp edges together to make a seal. Bake 10 to 15 minutes or until bags are puffed.

Number of Servings   4

PORK CHOPS WITH APRICOT SAUCE

SERVING SIZE
1/6th recipe (1 chop +
vegetables & sauce)

EXCHANGES
Vegetable   1
Meat, lean   3

PYRAMID SERVINGS
Vegetable   1
Meat   1

NUTRITION FACTS
Calories   203
Calories from Fat   74
Fat   8 g
  Saturated Fat   3 g
Cholesterol   69 mg
Sodium   77 mg
Carbohydrate   5 g
  Dietary Fiber   1 g
  Sugars   3 g
Protein   25 g

1/2 cup	ESTEE Apricot Fruit Spread
1 Tbsp	orange juice
1 tsp	crushed red pepper
6	(5- to 6-oz) lean center-loin pork chops (1/2 inch thick) Vegetable cooking spray
1 medium	green pepper, seeded and cut into julienne strips
1 medium	red pepper, seeded and cut into julienne strips
1/2 small	sweet onion, cut into thin slices and separated

1. Combine first 3 ingredients in a saucepan. Cook over medium heat until fruit spread melts, stirring constantly. Remove from heat.
2. Trim fat from pork chops. Coat a large non-stick skillet with cooking spray; place over medium-high heat until hot. Add chops and cook until browned on both sides. Drain and pat dry with paper towels. Transfer chops to a 12 x 8 x 2-inch baking dish. Brush chops with reserved apricot glaze, reserving any leftover glaze. Cover and bake at 350°F for 30 minutes. Add peppers and onions and bake, uncovered, an additional 15 minutes or until pork chops are tender, brushing frequently with reserved apricot glaze.

Number of Servings   6

BAKED STUFFED FISH FILLET

SERVING SIZE
1/4th recipe

EXCHANGES
Starch   1
Meat, very lean   3
Fat   1

PYRAMID SERVINGS
Starch   1
Meat   1

NUTRITION FACTS
Calories   230
Calories from Fat   61
Fat   7 g
    Saturated Fat   1 g
Cholesterol   61 mg
Sodium   89 mg
Carbohydrate   15 g
    Dietary Fiber   1 g
    Sugars   2 g
Protein   27 g

1 1/2 lbs	fresh fish fillets (haddock, cod, or pollock may be used)
1/4 cup	chopped onion
1 Tbsp	chopped fresh parsley
4 tsp	fresh lemon juice
1 tsp	garlic powder
1 tsp	paprika
2 Tbsp	unsalted margarine, melted
4 wedges	fresh lemon
2 cups	crushed GRAINFIELD's Whole Grain Crispy Brown Rice

1. Preheat oven to 350°F.
2. Wash and dry fish.
3. Combine Whole Grain Crispy Brown Rice, chopped onion, parsley, garlic, paprika, 1 Tbsp margarine, and lemon juice. Toss to moisten the Whole Grain Crispy Brown Rice.
4. Lightly grease a 13 x 9-inch baking dish. Put half of fish fillets into dish. Spoon stuffing mixture on fish. Top with remaining fillets. Brush fish with melted margarine. Dust with paprika.
5. Bake for 20 minutes or until fish flakes easily with fork. Remove from oven. Dust with paprika. Serve with wedge of lemon on the side.

Number of Servings   4

STUFFED BONELESS CHICKEN BREASTS

SERVING SIZE
1/4th recipe

EXCHANGES
Starch   1
Meat, lean   4
Fat   1 1/2

PYRAMID SERVINGS
Starch   1
Meat   1 1/2

NUTRITION FACTS
Calories   370
Calories from Fat   174
Fat   19 g
   Saturated Fat   6 g
Cholesterol   90 mg
Sodium   203 mg
Carbohydrate   11 g
   Dietary Fiber   1 g
   Sugars   1 g
Protein   37 g

4	boneless, skinless chicken breasts
4 Tbsp	salt-free butter or margarine
1 1/2 cups	chopped fresh mushrooms
1 cup	grated mozzarella or provolone cheese
2 tsp	mixed herbs (savory, sage, thyme, marjoram, rosemary)
1 1/2 cups	crushed GRAINFIELD's Distinctly Lite

1. Preheat oven to 350°F.
2. Wash chicken breasts and pat dry. Brush with melted butter inside cavity and outside. Toss chopped fresh mushrooms, grated cheese, and 1 tsp herbs together. Stuff mixture inside each breast. Fasten with toothpicks.
3. Mix GRAINFIELD's Distinctly Lite with remaining mixed herbs. Roll breasts in herbed flakes. Place in lightly buttered baking dish.
4. Bake 45 minutes.

Number of Servings   4

GOLDEN BAKED FISH

SERVING SIZE
1/6th recipe

EXCHANGES
Starch   1
Meat, very lean   3

PYRAMID SERVINGS
Starch   1
Meat   1

NUTRITION FACTS
Calories   190
Calories from Fat   31
Fat   3 g
   Saturated Fat   1 g
Cholesterol   72 mg
Sodium   81 mg
Carbohydrate   12 g
   Dietary Fiber   0 g
   Sugars   1 g
Protein   26 g

1 1/2 lbs.	fillets haddock, cod, flounder, or sole
3 Tbsp	unprocessed flour
1 tsp	parsley
1 tsp	onion powder
Dash	basil
1 large	egg, beaten
1	lemon
2 cups	GRAINFIELD's Wheat Flakes or Corn Flakes, crushed Nonstick vegetable spray

1. Wash fish; wipe dry. Mix flour with seasonings. Toss fish in seasoned flour. Crush GRAINFIELD's Wheat Flakes or Corn Flakes. Dip in egg and then in crushed cereal. Place in baking pan sprayed with nonstick vegetable spray.
2. Bake at 350°F for 1/2 hour or to desired doneness. Serve garnished with lemon slices.

Number of Servings   6

BAKED TUNA SUPREME

SERVING SIZE
1/2 recipe

EXCHANGES
Starch   1
Meat, very lean   3

PYRAMID SERVINGS
Starch   1
Meat   1

NUTRITION FACTS
Calories   195
Calories from Fat   31
Fat   3 g
  Saturated Fat   1 g
Cholesterol   138 mg
Sodium   130 mg
Carbohydrate   19 g
  Dietary Fiber   2 g
  Sugars   4 g
Protein   24 g

1 can	tuna in water (unsalted)
1 cup	chopped celery
1/2 cup	chopped onion
1 Tbsp	chopped parsley
1 cup	GRAINFIELD's Wheat Flakes and/or Corn Flakes, crushed finely
1	egg
1 Tbsp	unsalted mayonnaise (optional)

In large bowl, combine tuna, celery, onion, parsley, GRAINFIELD's Wheat Flakes and/or Corn Flakes, egg, and mayonnaise. Shape into loaf, and bake 1/2 hour at 350°F.

Number of Servings   2

CRISPY BAKED CHICKEN

SERVING SIZE
1/4th recipe

EXCHANGES
Starch   1
Meat, lean   5
Fat   1/2

PYRAMID SERVINGS
Starch   1
Meat   2

NUTRITION FACTS
Calories   381
Calories from Fat   177
Fat   20 g
   Saturated Fat   4 g
Cholesterol   108 mg
Sodium   114 mg
Carbohydrate   13 g
   Dietary Fiber   0 g
   Sugars   1 g
Protein   36 g

1	fryer chicken (cut up), skin removed
2 oz	unsalted butter or margarine
2 cups	GRAINFIELD's Corn Flakes, crushed
1 tsp	garlic, onion, celery powder, or seasonings desired

1. Wash and wipe chicken pieces. Melt butter or margarine over low heat, set aside. Pour GRAINFIELD's Corn Flakes into a plastic bag and crush with rolling pin. Mix in seasonings. Brush chicken with butter. Drop in bag, one or two pieces of chicken at a time. Shake to evenly coat.
2. Place in baking dish, and bake at 350°F for 1 hour.

Number of Servings   4

MEXICAN MEAT LOAF

SERVING SIZE
1/6th recipe

EXCHANGES
Starch   1
Meat, medium fat   3

PYRAMID SERVINGS
Starch   1
Meat   1

NUTRITION FACTS
Calories   289
Calories from Fat   143
Fat   16 g
    Saturated Fat   6 g
Cholesterol   105 mg
Sodium   79 mg
Carbohydrate   13 g
    Dietary Fiber   2 g
    Sugars   4 g
Protein   23 g

1	onion
1	pepper (green or red)
1 1/2 cups	chopped fresh mushrooms
1 clove	garlic, chopped fine
1 1/2 lb	lean ground beef
1	egg
1 1/2 cups	GRAINFIELD's Corn Flakes or Wheat Flakes crushed
1 tsp	black pepper
	Low-Salt Chili Sauce, p. 21

1. Sauté onion, pepper, mushrooms, and garlic until soft in a pan sprayed with nonstick vegetable spray.
2. Place ground beef in mixing bowl. Mix in sautéed vegetables, egg, GRAINFIELD's Corn Flakes or Wheat Flakes, and black pepper. Shape in loaf pan. Slash top of meat loaf
   3 or 4 times, and fill with chili sauce.
3. Bake 1 to 1 1/2 hours at 325–350°F. After baking, pour off any fat.

Number of Servings   6

15-MINUTE CHICKEN & RICE DINNER

SERVING SIZE
1/4th recipe

EXCHANGES
Starch   3
Meat, lean   4

PYRAMID SERVINGS
Starch   3
Meat   2

NUTRITION FACTS
(using water)
Calories   430
Calories from Fat 90
Fat   10 g
   Saturated Fat   2.5 g
Cholesterol   90 mg
Sodium   700 mg*
Carbohydrate   41 g
   Dietary Fiber   0 g
   Sugars   1 g
Protein   38 g

When you want food fast but not fast food, don't call the pizza place. Call on MINUTE Rice. With 15-Minute Chicken and Rice Dinner, you will have dinner on the table in, well, 15 minutes. Now that's dinner in no time!

1 Tbsp	oil
4	boneless, skinless chicken breast halves (about 1 1/4 lb)
1 can	(10 3/4 oz) condensed cream of chicken soup
1 soup can	(1 1/3 cups) water or skim milk
2 cups	MINUTE Original Rice, uncooked

1. Heat oil in large nonstick skillet on medium-high heat. Add chicken; cook 5 minutes on each side or until lightly browned. Remove from skillet.
2. Add soup and water to skillet. Bring to boil.
3. Stir in rice. Top with chicken; cover. Cook on low heat 5 minutes. Stir.

Number of Servings   4

* >400 mg of sodium

Reprinted with permission of Kraft Foods, Inc.

15-MINUTE CHICKEN & STUFFING SKILLET

SERVING SIZE
1/4th recipe

EXCHANGES
Starch   2
Meat, lean   4
Fat   1

PYRAMID SERVINGS
Starch   2
Meat   2

NUTRITION FACTS
Calories   420
Calories from Fat   130
Fat   15 g
  Saturated Fat   3 g
Cholesterol   85 mg
Sodium   620 mg*
Carbohydrate   31 g
  Dietary Fiber   1 g
  Sugars   4 g
Protein   38 g

4	boneless, skinless chicken breast halves (about 1 1/4 lb)
4 Tbsp	margarine, divided
1 pkg	(6 oz) STOVE TOP Lower Sodium Stuffing Mix for Chicken
1 1/3 cups	water

1. Brown chicken in 2 Tbsp of the margarine in large nonstick skillet.
2. Add contents of STOVE TOP vegetable/ seasoning packet, water, and remaining 2 Tbsp margarine. Bring to boil. Reduce heat to low; cover and simmer 5 minutes.
3. Stir stuffing crumbs into skillet; cover. Remove from heat. Let stand 5 minutes.

Number of Servings   4

* >400 mg of sodium

Reprinted with permission of Kraft Foods, Inc.

EASY CHICKEN FETTUCCINE

SERVING SIZE
1/6th recipe

EXCHANGES
Starch   2 1/2
Meat, lean   2

PYRAMID SERVINGS
Starch   2 1/2
Meat   1

NUTRITION FACTS
Calories   300
Calories from Fat   60
Fat   6 g
  Saturated Fat   1 g
Cholesterol   40 mg
Sodium   340 mg
Carbohydrate   38 g
  Dietary Fiber   2 g
  Sugars   4 g
Protein   21 g

8 oz	plain or spinach fettuccine
2	skinless boneless chicken breast halves (about 3/4 lb), cut into chunks
	Nonstick cooking spray
1/2 cup	skim milk
1/4 cup	soft reduced-calorie margarine
3/4 cup	(3 oz) KRAFT FREE Nonfat Grated Topping
3/4 tsp	garlic powder
1/4 tsp	pepper

1. Cook fettuccine as directed on package; drain. Meanwhile, cook chicken in skillet sprayed with nonstick cooking spray until cooked through.
2. Add milk and margarine to hot fettuccine.
3. Stir in chicken, Grated Topping, and seasonings.

Number of Servings   6

Reprinted with permission of Kraft Foods, Inc.

QUICK CHICKEN MARINARA

SERVING SIZE
1/4th recipe

EXCHANGES
Starch   3
Meat, very lean   3
Monounsat Fat   1

PYRAMID SERVINGS
Starch   2 1/2
Vegetable   1
Meat   1

NUTRITION FACTS
Calories   410
Calories from Fat   110
Fat   12 g
   Saturated Fat   2 g
Cholesterol   50 mg
Sodium   630 mg*
Carbohydrate   45 g
   Dietary Fiber   5 g
   Sugars   8 g
Protein   29 g

1 Tbsp	olive oil
2	boneless, skinless chicken breast halves (about 3/4 lb), cut into strips
1	yellow or green pepper, cut into strips
1 pkg	(15 oz) DI GIORNO Marinara Sauce
1 pkg	(9 oz) DI GIORNO Spinach Fettuccine, cooked, drained

1. Heat oil in skillet on medium-high heat. Add chicken and pepper; cook and stir 3 minutes. Stir in sauce. Cook on medium heat 3 to 5 minutes or until chicken is cooked through.
2. Serve over hot fettuccine. Top with DI GIORNO Shredded Parmesan Cheese, if desired.

Number of Servings   4

* >400 mg of sodium

Reprinted with permission of Kraft Foods, Inc.

BREAKFAST BURRITO

SERVING SIZE
1 burrito

EXCHANGES
Starch   1 1/2
Meat, medium fat   1
Fat   1

PYRAMID SERVINGS
Starch   1 1/2
Meat   1/2
Fat   1

NUTRITION FACTS
Calories   230
Calories from Fat   90
Fat   10 g
  Saturated Fat   3.5 g
Cholesterol   30 mg
Sodium   810 mg*
Carbohydrate   21 g
  Dietary Fiber   1 g
  Sugars   1 g
Protein   13 g

4 slices	LOUIS RICH Turkey Bacon
2	7-inch flour tortillas
2 Tbsp	KRAFT Natural Shredded Sharp Cheddar Cheese
2 large	egg whites
1 Tbsp	chopped chilies
	Salsa or taco sauce (optional)

1. Heat turkey bacon in nonstick skillet on medium heat 8 to 10 minutes or until lightly browned. Place 2 turkey bacon slices on each tortilla; sprinkle with cheese.
2. Beat egg whites and chilies together; add to hot skillet. Cook and stir 2 minutes or until set. Divide egg mixture between tortillas; fold tortillas over filling. Top with salsa, if desired.
3. **To keep warm**: Wrap filled burritos in foil and place in warm oven for up to 30 minutes

Number of Servings   2

* >400 mg of sodium

Reprinted with permission of Kraft Foods, Inc.

SATURDAY SKILLET BREAKFAST

SERVING SIZE
1/4th recipe

EXCHANGES
Starch   1/2
Meat, very lean   2
Fat   1

PYRAMID SERVINGS
Starch   1/2
Meat   1

NUTRITION FACTS
Calories   160
Calories from Fat   70
Fat   8 g
  Saturated Fat   2 g
Cholesterol   35 mg
Sodium   640 mg*
Carbohydrate   9 g
  Dietary Fiber   1 g
  Sugars   1 g
Protein   12 g

12 slices	LOUIS RICH Turkey Bacon, cut into 1/2-inch pieces
1 medium	potato, cut into small cubes
2	green onions, thinly sliced
1/2 tsp	chili powder
1 carton	(8 oz) frozen, thawed or refrigerated cholesterol-free egg product, beaten

1. Place turkey bacon and potato in nonstick skillet. Cook on medium heat 12 minutes or until potatoes are fork-tender, stirring frequently.
2. Stir in onions and chili powder. Pour egg product evenly over mixture; cover. Reduce heat to low and cook 5 minutes or until mixture is set. Cut into 4 wedges.

Number of Servings   4

* >400 mg of sodium

Reprinted with permission of Kraft Foods, Inc.

SHAKE 'N BAKE CHICKEN NUGGETS

SERVING SIZE
1/6th recipe

EXCHANGES
Starch   1/2
Meat, very lean   3
Fat   1/2

PYRAMID SERVINGS
Starch   1/2
Meat   1

NUTRITION FACTS
Calories   160
Calories from Fat   20
Fat   2.5 g
  Saturated Fat   0.5 g
Cholesterol   55 mg
Sodium   360 mg
Carbohydrate   9 g
  Dietary Fiber   0 g
  Sugars   1 g
Protein   24 g

It's time to fix your family's favorite dinner. You must be kidding! On a weeknight? Yes, even after you've worked all day, you can make your family's favorite dinner—SHAKE 'N BAKE Chicken Nuggets. Dinner from scratch is ready in a shake! Just cut chicken into chunks and let SHAKE 'N BAKE do the rest. Fifteen minutes in the oven and your family's favorite dinner is on the table with time left over to watch the evening news!

5	boneless, skinless chicken breast halves, cut into 1 1/2- to 2-inch pieces
1	packet SHAKE 'N BAKE Seasoning and Coating Mixture Original Recipe for Chicken

1. Shake chicken pieces with coating mixture; discard any remaining mixture.
2. Bake at 400°F for 10 to 15 minutes or until cooked through.

Number of Servings   6

Reprinted with permission of Kraft Foods, Inc.

SMOKED TURKEY CRUNCH SANDWICH

SERVING SIZE
1 sandwich

EXCHANGES
Starch   3
Meat, lean   1

PYRAMID SERVINGS
Starch   3
Meat   1/2

NUTRITION FACTS
Calories   340
Calories from Fat   50
Fat   6 g
  Saturated Fat   2.5 g
Cholesterol   25 mg
Sodium   1050 mg*
Carbohydrate   55 g
  Dietary Fiber   4 g
  Sugars   15 g
Protein   17 g

2 slices	bran bread
1 Tbsp	PHILADELPHIA BRAND Neufchatel 1/3 Less Fat Than Cream Cheese
2 tsp	low-sugar strawberry spread
4	thin wedges Granny Smith apple (about 1/4 apple)
2 slices	LOUIS RICH Fat Free Hickory Smoked Turkey Breast

1. Spread 1 slice bran bread with Neufchatel cheese. Layer with turkey breast and apple wedges.
2. Top with remaining slice of bread spread with strawberry spread.

Number of Servings   1

* >400 mg of sodium

Reprinted with permission of Kraft Foods, Inc.

CREAMY CHICKEN BROCCOLI BAKE

SERVING SIZE
1/6th recipe

EXCHANGES
Starch   2
Meat, lean   4
Saturated Fat   1/2

PYRAMID SERVINGS
Starch   2
Meat   2

NUTRITION FACTS
Calories   380
Calories from Fat   130
Fat   14 g
    Saturated Fat   8 g
Cholesterol   90 mg
Sodium   810 mg*
Carbohydrate   29 g
    Dietary Fiber   1 g
    Sugars   8 g
Protein   33 g

4	boneless, skinless chicken breast halves (about 1 1/4 lb), cubed
1 1/2 cups	MINUTE Original Rice, uncooked
1 1/4 cups	skim milk
1 pkg	(10 oz) frozen chopped broccoli, thawed, drained
1/2 lb	(8 oz) VELVEETA Pasteurized Process Cheese Spread, cut up
1/2 cup	MIRACLE WHIP LIGHT Dressing

1. Mix all ingredients.
2. Spoon into 12 x 8-inch baking dish.
3. Bake at 375°F for 30 minutes or until chicken is cooked through.

Number of Servings   6

---

* >400 mg of sodium

Reprinted with permission of Kraft Foods, Inc.

Date Bran Muffins, page 157; Date Nut Twist, page 158; Apricot-Almond Coffee Ring, page 156.

Creamy
Vegetable
Medley,
page 33

Fiesta
Chicken
Soup,
page 63

Glazed
Fruit Salad,
page 36

Sweet and
Sour
Chicken,
page 128

Deb's Dilly Dip, page 25

SHAKE 'N BAKE Chicken Nuggets, page 110

15-Minute
Chicken
and Rice,
page 104

Creamy
Ranch and
Parmesan
Chicken
Salad,
page 113

Tangy
Broccoli
Salad,
page 58

Tangy
Broiled
Chicken,
page 82
and Bloody
Eight,
page 4

Stuffed
Pepper
Casserole,
page 61

Pork Chops
with Apple
Raisin
Stuffing,
page 118

Saturday
Skillet
Breakfast,
page 109

Cherry
Lattice Pie,
page 147
and
Nectarine
and Berry
Pie, page
148

CREAMY RANCH & PARMESAN CHICKEN SALAD

SERVING SIZE
2 cups

EXCHANGES
Starch   1 1/2
Vegetable   1
Meat, very lean   3

PYRAMID SERVINGS
Starch   1 1/2
Vegetable   1
Meat   1

NUTRITION FACTS
Calories   250
Calories from Fat   35
Fat   4 g
Saturated Fat   1 g
Cholesterol   60 mg
Sodium   790 mg*
Carbohydrate   28 g
Dietary Fiber   3 g
Sugars   6 g
Protein   25 g

4	boneless, skinless chicken breast halves (about 1 1/4 lb), cut into strips
1 cup	KRAFT FREE Ranch Fat Free Dressing,† divided
1/2 cup	(2 oz) KRAFT FREE Nonfat Grated Topping‡
	Nonstick cooking spray
1 pkg	(10 oz) salad greens
1 cup	cherry tomatoes
1 cup	seasoned croutons
1	red, yellow, or green pepper, cut into strips

1. Toss chicken with 1/4 cup of the dressing; coat with grated topping.
2. Cook chicken in large skillet sprayed with nonstick cooking spray on medium heat 10 minutes or until cooked through.
3. Toss chicken and remaining ingredients lightly with remaining dressing.

Number of Servings   6

* >400 mg of sodium
† Or use KRAFT Ranch Dressing
‡ Or use KRAFT 100% Grated Parmesan Cheese

Reprinted with permission of Kraft Foods, Inc.

113

GREEK CHICKEN SALAD

SERVING SIZE
1 1/2 cups

EXCHANGES
Carbohydrate   1/2
Vegetable   1
Meat, very lean   2
Fat   1

PYRAMID SERVINGS
Sweet   1/2
Vegetable   1
Meat   1

NUTRITION FACTS
Calories   200
Calories from Fat   60
Fat   7 g
   Saturated Fat   3.5 g
Cholesterol   55 mg
Sodium   730 mg*
Carbohydrate   11 g
   Dietary Fiber   2 g
   Sugars   7 g
Protein   23 g

1 cup	KRAFT FREE Italian Fat Free Dressing
1 tsp	dried oregano leaves, crushed
1 lb	boneless, skinless chicken breasts, cut into strips
1 pkg	(10 oz) salad greens
1 pkg	(4 oz) ATHENOS Crumbled Feta Cheese
3	plum tomatoes, sliced
1/2	cucumber, seeded, sliced, and quartered
1/2 cup	thinly sliced red onion
1 can	(2 1/4 oz) pitted ripe olives, drained

1. Mix dressing and oregano. Cook chicken in 3 Tbsp of the dressing mixture in large skillet on medium heat 10 minutes or until cooked through.
2. Toss remaining ingredients with remaining dressing mixture. Place on serving platter. Arrange chicken over greens mixture.

Number of Servings   6

---

* >400 mg of sodium

Reprinted with permission of Kraft Foods, Inc.

HAM SANDWICH WITH NECTARINE SALSA

SERVING SIZE
1 sandwich

EXCHANGES
Starch   1 1/2
Meat, very lean   1

PYRAMID SERVINGS
Starch   1 1/2
Meat   1/2

NUTRITION FACTS
Calories   160
Calories from Fat   10
Fat   1 g
  Saturated Fat   0 g
Cholesterol   15 mg
Sodium   840 mg*
Carbohydrate   26 g
  Dietary Fiber   2 g
  Sugars   7 g
Protein   11 g

2 Tbsp	KRAFT Mayo Fat Free Mayonnaise Dressing
1/2 tsp	fresh lime juice
Dash	ground red pepper
1	nectarine, coarsely chopped
2 Tbsp	coarsely chopped sweet onion
1 Tbsp	coarsely chopped cilantro
3	pita bread halves
3	lettuce leaves
1 pkg	(5 oz) OSCAR MAYER FREE Fat Free DELI-THIN Honey Baked, Cooked, or Smoked Cooked Ham

1. Mix dressing, lime juice, and red pepper until combined. Stir in nectarine, sweet onion, and cilantro to make salsa.
2. Fill each pita bread half with lettuce, 3 ham slices, and 1/3 of the salsa mixture.

Number of Servings   3

* >400 mg of sodium

Reprinted with permission of Kraft Foods, Inc.

VEGETABLE TURKEY POCKETS

SERVING SIZE
1/4th recipe

EXCHANGES
Starch   1
Vegetable   1
Meat, medium fat   1
Polyunsat Fat   1

PYRAMID SERVINGS
Starch   2
Vegetable   1
Meat   1

NUTRITION FACTS
Calories   220
Calories from Fat   90
Fat   10 g
   Saturated Fat   1.5 g
Cholesterol   20 mg
Sodium   850 mg*
Carbohydrate   24 g
   Dietary Fiber   1 g
   Sugars   4 g
Protein   10 g

1/4 cup	SEVEN SEAS VIVA 1/3 Less Fat Ranch Reduced Calorie Dressing
1/4 cup	KRAFT Mayo Light Mayonnaise
1 1/2 cups	LOUIS RICH Oven-Roasted Breast of Turkey strips
1/2 cup	chopped cucumber
1/2 cup	shredded carrot
1 small	tomato, chopped
1 tsp	dried basil leaves, crushed
2	pita breads, cut in half

1. Mix dressing and mayonnaise until combined. Stir in turkey, cucumber, carrot, tomato, and basil. Refrigerate.
2. Fill bread with turkey mixture.

Number of Servings   4

---

* >400 mg of sodium

Reprinted with permission of Kraft Foods, Inc.

CHILI CORN PIE

SERVING SIZE
1/6th recipe

EXCHANGES
Starch   2 1/2
Meat, medium fat   2
Saturated Fat   1 1/2

PYRAMID SERVINGS
Starch   2 1/2
Meat   1
Fat   1 1/2

NUTRITION FACTS
Calories   419
Calories from Fat   168
Fat   19 g
   Saturated Fat   8 g
Cholesterol   67 mg
Sodium   1039 mg*
Carbohydrate   39 g
   Dietary Fiber   4 g
   Sugars   5 g
Protein   23 g

4 cups	PEPPERIDGE FARM Corn Bread Stuffing
1 can	(14 1/2 oz) SWANSON Chicken Broth†
1 lb	lean ground beef
1 medium	onion, coarsely chopped (about 1/2 cup)
1 Tbsp	chili powder
1/4 tsp	garlic powder
1 can	(8 oz) whole kernel corn, drained
1 cup	shredded cheddar cheese (4 oz)
1/4 cup	PACE Thick & Chunky Salsa
	Sour Cream (optional)

1. Lightly mix stuffing and broth. Let stand 5 minutes or until broth is absorbed. Set aside 1/2 cup stuffing mixture. Press remaining stuffing mixture into greased 9-inch pie plate to form crust. Bake at 350°F for 15 minutes.

2. In medium skillet over medium-high heat, cook beef, onion, chili powder, and garlic powder until beef is browned, stirring to separate meat. Pour off fat. Add corn, cheese, salsa, and reserved stuffing mixture. Spoon into crust.

3. Bake 10 minutes more or until hot. Serve with sour cream. If desired, garnish with cherry tomato and jalapeño pepper.

Number of Servings   6

* >400 mg of sodium
†Use SWANSON NATURAL GOODNESS Chicken Broth to lower sodium in the recipe.

Recipe provided courtesy of Campbell Soup Company.

PORK CHOPS WITH APPLE RAISIN STUFFING

SERVING SIZE
1 pork chop +
1/4 stuffing

EXCHANGES
Starch   3 1/2
Meat, lean   3

PYRAMID SERVINGS
Starch   3
Fruit   1/2
Meat   1

NUTRITION FACTS
Calories   468
Calories from Fat   92
Fat   10 g
   Saturated Fat   3 g
Cholesterol   71 mg
Sodium   934 mg*
Carbohydrate   55 g
   Dietary Fiber   5 g
   Sugars   11 g
Protein   32 g

1 cup	applesauce, unsweetened
1/2 cup	water
2 Tbsp	margarine or butter, melted
1 stalk	celery, chopped (about 1/2 cup)
2 Tbsp	raisins
4 cups	PEPPERIDGE FARM Herb Seasoned Stuffing
4	boneless pork chops, 3/4 inch thick (about 1 lb) Paprika or ground cinnamon

1. Mix applesauce, water, margarine, celery and raisins. Add stuffing. Mix lightly. Spoon into 2-qt shallow baking dish. Arrange chops over stuffing. Sprinkle paprika over chops.
2. Bake at 400°F for 35 minutes or until chops are no longer pink. If desired, garnish with apple, fresh chives, and fresh sage.

Number of Servings   4

* >400 mg of sodium

Recipe provided courtesy of Campbell Soup Company.

LEMON-HERB FISH BAKE

SERVING SIZE
1/6th recipe

EXCHANGES
Starch   2
Meat, very lean   4
Fat   1

PYRAMID SERVINGS
Starch   2
Meat   2

NUTRITION FACTS
Calories   357
Calories from Fat   91
Fat   10 g
Saturated Fat   2 g
Cholesterol   36 mg
Sodium   699 mg*
Carbohydrate   33 g
Dietary Fiber   4 g
Sugars   3 g
Protein   28 g

1 cup	water†
4 Tbsp	margarine or butter
2 medium	carrots, sliced (about 1 cup)
1 small	green pepper, chopped (about 1/2 cup)
4 cups	PEPPERIDGE FARM Herb Seasoned Stuffing
1 1/2 lb	fresh or thawed frozen firm white fish fillets (cod, haddock, or halibut)
1 Tbsp	lemon juice
1 Tbsp	chopped fresh parsley or 1 tsp dried parsley flakes

1. In medium saucepan, mix water, 2 Tbsp margarine, carrots, and pepper. Over medium-high heat, heat to a boil. Remove from heat. Add stuffing. Mix lightly.
2. Spoon stuffing across center of 3-qt shallow baking dish, leaving space on both sides for fish. Arrange fish on each side of stuffing.
3. Melt remaining margarine and mix with lemon juice and parsley. Spoon over fish.
4. Bake at 400°F for 15 minutes or until fish flakes easily when tested with a fork.

Number of Servings   6

* >400 mg of sodium
† For more moist stuffing, increase water by 2 to 4 Tbsp.

Recipe provided courtesy of Campbell Soup Company.

BEEFY VEGETABLE SKILLET

SERVING SIZE
1/4th recipe

EXCHANGES
Starch   1 1/2
Vegetable   1
Meat, medium fat   3

PYRAMID SERVINGS
Starch   1 1/2
Vegetable   1
Meat   1

NUTRITION FACTS
Calories   366
Calories from Fat   150
Fat   17 g
   Saturated Fat   7 g
Cholesterol   72 mg
Sodium   724 mg*
Carbohydrate   30 g
   Dietary Fiber   3 g
   Sugars   6 g
Protein   25 g

1 lb	lean ground beef
1 medium	onion, chopped (about 1/2 cup)
2 medium	zucchini, quartered lengthwise and sliced
1 can	(about 14 1/2 oz) stewed tomatoes
2 cups	PEPPERIDGE FARM Cubed Herb Seasoned Stuffing
2 Tbsp	grated Parmesan cheese

1. In medium skillet over medium-high heat, cook beef and onion until beef is browned, stirring to separate meat. Pour off fat.
2. Add zucchini and tomatoes. Heat to a boil. Reduce heat to low. Cover and cook 5 minutes or until zucchini is tender, stirring occasionally. Remove from heat.
3. Add stuffing and cheese. Mix lightly. Cover and let stand 5 minutes.

Number of Servings   4

* >400 mg of sodium

Recipe provided courtesy of Campbell Soup Company.

HERBED CRAB CAKES

SERVING SIZE
1/6th recipe

EXCHANGES
Starch   1
Meat, medium fat   2
Fat   1

PYRAMID SERVINGS
Starch   1
Meat   1
Fat   1/2

NUTRITION FACTS
Calories   263
Calories from Fat   143
Fat   16 g
    Saturated Fat   3 g
Cholesterol   130 mg
Sodium   558 mg*
Carbohydrate   12 g
    Dietary Fiber   1 g
    Sugars   1 g
Protein   16 g

1 1/2 cups	PEPPERIDGE FARM Herb Seasoned Stuffing
2	eggs, beaten
1/3 cup	mayonnaise
2 tsp	Dijon-style mustard
1 tsp	Worcestershire sauce
1 Tbsp	chopped fresh parsley or 1 tsp dried parsley flakes
1 can	(16 oz) refrigerated pasteurized crab meat
2 Tbsp	margarine or butter Lemon wedges

1. Finely crush 1/2 cup stuffing. Set aside.
2. Lightly mix remaining stuffing, eggs, mayonnaise, mustard, Worcestershire, parsley, and crab meat. Shape firmly into 6 patties, 1/2 inch thick. Coat with reserved stuffing.
3. In medium skillet over medium heat, heat margarine. Cook patties in 2 batches 5 minutes or until hot.† Serve with lemon wedges.

Number of Servings   6

* >400 mg of sodium
† Use additional margarine if necessary.

Recipe provided courtesy of Campbell Soup Company.

HAM AND ASPARAGUS STRATA

SERVING SIZE
1/8th recipe

EXCHANGES
Starch   1 1/2
Meat, medium fat   3

PYRAMID SERVINGS
Starch   1 1/2
Meat   1

NUTRITION FACTS
Calories   344
Calories from Fat   140
Fat   16 g
   Saturated Fat   7 g
Cholesterol   173 mg
Sodium   992 mg*
Carbohydrate   27 g
   Dietary Fiber   2 g
   Sugars   6 g
Protein   25 g

4 cups	PEPPERIDGE FARM Cubed Country Style Stuffing
2 cups	shredded Swiss cheese (8 oz)
1 1/2 cups	cooked cut asparagus
1 1/2 cups	cubed cooked ham
1 can	(10 3/4 oz) CAMPBELL'S condensed Cream of Asparagus Soup
2 cups	skim milk
5	eggs, beaten
1 Tbsp	Dijon-style mustard

1. Mix stuffing, cheese, asparagus, and ham. Spoon into greased 3-qt shallow baking dish.
2. Mix soup, milk, eggs, and mustard. Pour over stuffing mixture.
3. Bake at 350°F for 45 minutes or until knife inserted near center comes out clean. Let stand 5 minutes. If desired, garnish with fresh oregano.

Tip: For 1 1/2 cups cooked cut asparagus, use 3/4 lb asparagus, trimmed and cut into 1-inch pieces, or 1 pkg (about 10 oz) frozen asparagus spears, thawed, drained, and cut into 1-inch pieces.

Number of Servings   8

* >400 mg of sodium

Recipe provided courtesy of Campbell Soup Company.

SZECHUAN SHRIMP

SERVING SIZE
1/4th recipe

EXCHANGES
Starch   3 1/2
Meat, very lean   2

PYRAMID SERVINGS
Starch   3 1/2
Meat   1

NUTRITION FACTS
Calories   329
Calories from Fat   11
Fat   1 g
   Saturated Fat   0 g
Cholesterol   161 mg
Sodium   646 mg*
Carbohydrate   54 g
   Dietary Fiber   1 g
   Sugars   2 g
Protein   22 g

3 Tbsp	cornstarch
1 can	(14 1/2 oz) SWANSON Oriental Broth
1/2 tsp	garlic powder
1/4 tsp	crushed red pepper
4	green onions, cut into 1-inch pieces (about 1 cup)
1 lb	medium shrimp, shelled and deveined
4 cups	hot, cooked rice, cooked without salt

1. In medium saucepan, mix cornstarch, broth, garlic powder, pepper, and onions. Over medium-high heat, cook until mixture boils and thickens, stirring constantly.
2. Add shrimp. Cook 5 minutes or until shrimp turn pink, stirring often. Serve over rice.

Number of Servings   4

* >400 mg of sodium

Recipe provided courtesy of Campbell Soup Company.

GARLIC PORK KABOBS

SERVING SIZE
1 kabob + sauce +
1 cup rice

EXCHANGES
Starch   4
Meat, very lean   3

PYRAMID SERVINGS
Starch   4
Meat   1
Vegetable   1

NUTRITION FACTS
Calories   436
Calories from Fat   46
   Saturated Fat   2 g
Cholesterol   71 mg
Sodium   558 mg*
Carbohydrate   63 g
   Dietary Fiber   3 g
   Sugars   11 g
Protein   32 g

2 Tbsp	cornstarch
1 can	(14 1/2 oz) SWANSON Oriental Broth
2 cloves	garlic, minced
1 Tbsp	packed brown sugar
1 Tbsp	ketchup
2 tsp	vinegar
4	long skewers
1 lb	boneless pork loin, cut into 1-inch cubes
12 medium	mushrooms
1 large	red onion, cut into 12 wedges
4	cherry tomatoes
4 cups	hot, cooked rice, cooked without salt

1. In small saucepan, mix cornstarch, broth, garlic, sugar, ketchup, and vinegar until smooth. Over medium heat, cook until mixture boils and thickens, stirring constantly.
2. On 4 long skewers, thread pork, mushrooms, and onion alternately.
3. Place kabobs on lightly oiled grill rack over medium-hot coals. Grill uncovered 20 minutes or until pork is no longer pink, turning and brushing often with broth mixture.
4. Place one tomato on end of each skewer.
5. Heat remaining broth mixture to a boil. Serve with kabobs and rice.

Number of Servings   4

* >400 mg of sodium

Recipe provided courtesy of Campbell Soup Company.

ORIENTAL CHICKEN AND VEGETABLE STIR-FRY

SERVING SIZE
1/4th recipe

EXCHANGES
Starch   3 1/2
Vegetable   1
Meat, very lean   3

PYRAMID SERVINGS
Starch   3 1/2
Vegetable   1
Meat   1

NUTRITION FACTS
Calories   404
Calories from Fat   31
Fat   3 g
   Saturated Fat   1 g
Cholesterol   69 mg
Sodium   560 mg*
Carbohydrate   59 g
   Dietary Fiber   4 g
   Sugars   6 g
Protein   32 g

2 Tbsp	cornstarch
1 can	(14 1/2 oz) SWANSON Oriental Broth
1 lb	skinless, boneless chicken breasts, cut into strips
5 cups	cut-up vegetables†
4 cups	hot, cooked rice, cooked without salt

1. In bowl mix cornstarch and 1 cup broth until smooth. Set aside.
2. In medium nonstick skillet over medium-high heat, stir-fry chicken in 2 batches until browned. Set chicken aside.
3. Add remaining broth and vegetables. Heat to a boil. Reduce heat to low.
4. Cover and cook 5 minutes or until vegetables are tender-crisp.
5. Stir cornstarch mixture and add. Cook until mixture boils and thickens, stirring constantly. Return chicken to pan and heat through. Serve over rice. If desired, garnish with radishes and red pepper.

Number of Servings   4

* >400 mg of sodium
† Use a combination of broccoli florets, green onions cut in l-inch pieces, sliced celery, and sliced carrot.

Recipe provided courtesy of Campbell Soup Company.

EASY CHICKEN PAPRIKASH

SERVING SIZE
1/4th recipe

EXCHANGES
Starch   3 1/2
Meat, very lean   4

PYRAMID SERVINGS
Starch   3 1/2
Meat   1 1/2

NUTRITION FACTS
Calories   410
Calories from Fat   59
Fat   7 g
   Saturated Fat   2 g
Cholesterol   123 mg
Sodium   513 mg*
Carbohydrate   51 g
   Dietary Fiber   3 g
   Sugars   6 g
Protein   36 g

4	skinless, boneless chicken breast halves (about 1 lb)
1 can	(14 1/2 oz) SWANSON Chicken Broth
1/4 cup	all-purpose flour
2 tsp	paprika
1/8 tsp	ground red pepper
1 medium	onion, sliced (about 1/2 cup)
1/3 cup	plain nonfat yogurt
4 cups	hot, cooked wide egg noodles (about 4 cups dry), cooked without salt

1. In medium nonstick skillet over medium-high heat, cook chicken 10 minutes or until browned. Set chicken aside.
2. In same pan gradually mix broth into flour, paprika, and pepper until smooth. Cook until mixture boils and thickens, stirring constantly. Return chicken to pan. Add onion. Reduce heat to low. Cover and cook 5 minutes or until chicken is no longer pink.
3. Remove from heat. Stir in yogurt. Serve with noodles. If desired, garnish with fresh parsley and tomato.

Number of Servings   4

* >400 mg of sodium

Recipe provided courtesy of Campbell Soup Company.

HONEY MUSTARD CHICKEN

SERVING SIZE
1/4th recipe

EXCHANGES
Starch   4
Meat, very lean   3

PYRAMID SERVINGS
Starch   4
Meat   1
Vegetable   1

NUTRITION FACTS
Calories   412
Calories from Fat   31
Fat   3 g
  Saturated Fat   1 g
Cholesterol   69 mg
Sodium   371 mg
Carbohydrate   60 g
  Dietary Fiber   2 g
  Sugars   8 g
Protein   31 g

2 Tbsp	cornstarch
1 can	(14 1/2 oz) SWANSON Chicken Broth
1 Tbsp	honey
1 Tbsp	Dijon-style or coarse-grain mustard
4	skinless, boneless chicken breast halves (about 1 lb)
1 large	carrot, cut into 2-inch match-stick-thin strips (about 1 cup)
1 medium	yellow or red onion, cut into wedges
4 cups	hot, cooked rice, cooked without salt

1. In bowl mix cornstarch, broth, honey, and mustard until smooth. Set aside.
2. In medium nonstick skillet over medium-high heat, cook chicken 10 minutes or until browned. Set chicken aside.
3. Stir cornstarch mixture and add. Cook until mixture boils and thickens, stirring constantly. Return chicken to pan. Add carrot and onion. Reduce heat to low. Cover and cook 5 minutes or until chicken is no longer pink. Serve with rice. If desired, garnish with green onion.

Number of Servings   4

Recipe provided courtesy of Campbell Soup Company.

SWEET AND SOUR CHICKEN

SERVING SIZE
1/4th recipe

EXCHANGES
Starch   4 1/2
Vegetable   1
Meat, very lean   2

PYRAMID SERVINGS
Starch   3 1/2
Vegetable   1
Meat   1

NUTRITION FACTS
Calories   453
Calories from Fat   30
Fat   3 g
  Saturated Fat   1 g
Cholesterol   69 mg
Sodium   523 mg*
Carbohydrate   73 g
  Dietary Fiber   2 g
  Sugars   21 g
Protein   30 g

3 Tbsp	cornstarch
1 can	(14 1/2 oz) SWANSON Oriental Broth
1/4 cup	vinegar
1/4 cup	sugar
1 lb	skinless, boneless chicken breasts, cut into cubes
1 small	green and/or red pepper, cut into 2-inch-long strips (about 1 cup)
1 medium	carrot, sliced (about 1/2 cup)
1 can	(about 8 oz) pineapple chunks in juice, drained
4 cups	hot, cooked rice, cooked without salt

1. In bowl mix cornstarch, broth, vinegar, and sugar until smooth. Set aside.
2. In medium nonstick skillet over medium-high heat, stir-fry chicken in 2 batches until browned. Set chicken aside.
3. Stir cornstarch mixture and add. Cook until mixture boils and thickens, stirring constantly. Return chicken to pan. Add pepper, carrot, and pineapple. Reduce heat to low. Cover and cook 5 minutes or until chicken is no longer pink. Serve over rice. If desired, garnish with fresh chives.

Sweet and Sour Pork:
Substitute 1 lb boneless pork loin, cut into cubes for chicken.

Number of Servings   4

* >400 mg of sodium

Recipe provided courtesy of Campbell Soup Company.

CHICKEN PASTA SALAD

SERVING SIZE
1/4th recipe

EXCHANGES
Starch   2
Vegetable   1
Meat, very lean   4
Fat   1/2

PYRAMID SERVINGS
Starch   2
Meat   2
Vegetable   1

NUTRITION FACTS
Calories   353
Calories from Fat   69
Fat   8 g
    Saturated Fat   3 g
Cholesterol   68 mg
Sodium   457 mg*
Carbohydrate   37 g
    Dietary Fiber   4 g
    Sugars   8 g
Protein   32 g

1 can	(14 1/2 oz) SWANSON NATURAL GOODNESS Chicken Broth
1/2 cup	plain nonfat yogurt
1/4 cup	grated Parmesan cheese
1 tsp	dried dill weed or dried basil leaves, crushed
3 cups	hot, cooked corkscrew macaroni (about 2 1/2 cups dry), cooked without salt
1 cup	cherry tomatoes cut in half
1 cup	frozen peas
1/2 cup	sliced mushrooms (about 2 oz)
1 small	red onion, chopped (about 1/2 cup)
2 cups	cubed cooked chicken Lettuce leaves

1. In medium bowl, mix broth, yogurt, cheese, and dill weed with fork.
2. In large shallow nonmetallic dish, toss macaroni, tomatoes, peas, mushrooms, onion, chicken, and broth mixture until evenly coated. Refrigerate at least 4 hours or overnight, stirring occasionally. Serve on lettuce. If desired, garnish with additional tomato.

Number of Servings   4

* >400 mg of sodium

Recipe provided courtesy of Campbell Soup Company.

QUICK CHILI AND RICE

SERVING SIZE
1/8th recipe

EXCHANGES
Starch   5
Meat, very lean   2
Fat   1

PYRAMID SERVINGS
Starch   4 1/2
Vegetable   1
Meat   1

NUTRITION FACTS
Calories   522
Calories from Fat   122
Fat   14 g
  Saturated Fat   5 g
Cholesterol   57 mg
Sodium   668 mg*
Carbohydrate   74 g
  Dietary Fiber   7 g
  Sugars   12 g
Protein   25 g

1 1/2 lb	lean ground beef (85% lean)
1 large	onion, chopped (about 1 cup)
2 Tbsp	chili powder
1/4 tsp	ground red pepper
3 cups	V8 100% Vegetable Juice
2 cans	(16 oz each) CAMPBELL'S Pork & Beans in Tomato Sauce
8 cups	hot, cooked rice, cooked without salt

1. In Dutch oven over medium-high heat, cook beef, onion, chili powder, and pepper until beef is browned, stirring to separate meat. Pour off fat.
2. Add "V8" juice and beans. Heat to a boil. Reduce heat to low. Cook 10 minutes, stirring occasionally. Serve over rice. If desired, garnish with green onion.

Number of Servings   8

* >400 mg of sodium

Recipe provided courtesy of Campbell Soup Company.

BEAN AND RICE BURRITOS

SERVING SIZE
1 burrito

EXCHANGES
PYRAMID SERVINGS
Starch   3
Fat   1/2

NUTRITION FACTS
Calories   272
Calories from Fat   48
Fat   5 g
  Saturated Fat   2 g
Cholesterol   8 mg
Sodium   540 mg*
Carbohydrate   48 g
  Dietary Fiber   5 g
  Sugars   7 g
Protein   9 g

	Vegetable cooking spray
1 medium	onion, chopped (about 1/2 cup)
1 can	(16 oz) CAMPBELL'S Pork & Beans in Tomato Sauce
1/3 cup	PACE Thick & Chunky Salsa
1/4 cup	shredded cheddar cheese (1 oz)
1 1/2 cups	cooked rice, cooked without salt
6	8-inch flour tortillas

1. Spray medium saucepan with cooking spray and heat over medium heat 1 minute. Add onion and cook until tender.
2. Add beans, salsa, cheese, and rice. Heat through, stirring occasionally.
3. Warm tortillas according to package directions. Spoon 1/2 cup bean mixture down center of each tortilla. Fold tortilla around filling.

Number of Servings   6

* >400 mg of sodium

Recipe provided courtesy of Campbell Soup Company.

QUICK CHICKEN AND NOODLES

SERVING SIZE
1/4th recipe

EXCHANGES
Starch   1
Vegetable   1
Meat, very lean   4

PYRAMID SERVINGS
Starch   1
Vegetable   1
Meat   2

NUTRITION FACTS
Calories   247
Calories from Fat   44
Fat   5 g
  Saturated Fat   1 g
Cholesterol   91 mg
Sodium   504 mg*
Carbohydrate   19 g
  Dietary Fiber   2 g
  Sugars   2 g
Protein   30 g

4	skinless, boneless chicken breast halves (about 1 lb)
1/4 tsp	garlic powder
1/8 tsp	paprika
1 can	(14 1/2 oz) SWANSON Chicken Broth
1/2 tsp	dried basil leaves, crushed
1/8 tsp	pepper
2 cups	frozen vegetable combination (broccoli, cauliflower, carrots)
2 cups	dry wide egg noodles

1. In medium nonstick skillet over medium-high heat, cook chicken 10 minutes or until browned. Sprinkle with garlic powder and paprika. Set chicken aside.
2. Add broth, basil, pepper, and vegetables. Heat to a boil. Stir in noodles. Return chicken to pan. Reduce heat to low. Cover and cook 10 minutes or until chicken is no longer pink. If desired, garnish with fresh basil.

Number of Servings   4

* >400 mg of sodium

Recipe provided courtesy of Campbell Soup Company.

SMOTHERED PORK CHOPS

SERVING SIZE
1/6th recipe

EXCHANGES
Starch   3
Meat, lean   3

PYRAMID SERVINGS
Starch   3
Meat   1

NUTRITION FACTS
Calories   385
Calories from Fat   85
Fat   9 g
    Saturated Fat   3 g
Cholesterol   111 mg
Sodium   285 mg
Carbohydrate   44 g
    Dietary Fiber   2 g
    Sugars   3 g
Protein   29 g

2 Tbsp	cornstarch
1 can	(14 1/2 oz) SWANSON Beef Broth
1/8 tsp	pepper
	Vegetable cooking spray
6	pork chops, 1/2 inch thick (about 1 1/2 lb)
1 medium	onion, sliced (about 1/2 cup)
6 cups	hot, cooked medium egg noodles (about 6 cups dry), cooked without salt

1. In bowl mix cornstarch, broth, and pepper until smooth. Set aside.
2. Spray medium skillet with cooking spray and heat over medium-high heat 1 minute. Add chops in 2 batches and cook 10 minutes or until browned. Set chops aside.
3. Remove pan from heat. Spray with cooking spray. Reduce heat to medium. Add onion and cook until tender-crisp.
4. Stir cornstarch mixture and add. Cook until mixture boils and thickens, stirring constantly. Return chops to pan. Reduce heat to low. Cover and cook 5 minutes or until chops are no longer pink. Serve with noodles.

Number of Servings   6

Recipe provided courtesy of Campbell Soup Company.

FISH STEAKS DIJON

SERVING SIZE
1/6th recipe

EXCHANGES
Meat, very lean   3
Fat   1/2

PYRAMID SERVINGS
Meat   1

NUTRITION FACTS
Calories   144
Calories from Fat   44
Fat   5 g
  Saturated Fat   1 g
Cholesterol   43 mg
Sodium   302 mg
Carbohydrate   2 g
  Dietary Fiber   0 g
  Sugars   0 g
Protein   22 g

1 can	(14 1/2 oz) SWANSON Chicken Broth
1 Tbsp	Dijon-style mustard
1 tsp	lemon juice
1/8 tsp	pepper
1 1/2 lb	swordfish steaks, 1 inch thick
1 Tbsp	cornstarch

1. Mix broth, mustard, lemon juice, and pepper. Pour 1 cup broth mixture into large, shallow, nonmetallic dish. Add fish and turn to coat. Cover and refrigerate 1 hour, turning fish occasionally.
2. In small saucepan mix, cornstarch and remaining broth mixture until smooth. Set aside.
3. Remove fish from marinade and place on lightly oiled grill rack over medium-hot coals. Grill uncovered 10 minutes or until fish flakes easily when tested with a fork, turning once and brushing often with marinade. Discard marinade.
4. Over medium heat, heat cornstarch mixture until mixture boils and thickens, stirring constantly. Serve with fish. If desired, garnish with cracked pepper.

Broiled Fish Steaks Dijon
Prepare as in first and second steps. In third step, remove fish from marinade and place on rack in broiler pan. Broil 4 inches from heat 10 minutes or until fish flakes easily when tested with a fork, turning once and brushing often with marinade. Discard marinade. Proceed as in fourth step.

Number of Servings   6

Recipe provided courtesy of Campbell Soup Company.

BEEF AND PASTA

SERVING SIZE
1/4th recipe

EXCHANGES
Starch   2
Meat, lean   2
Fat   1/2

PYRAMID SERVINGS
Starch   1 1/2
Vegetable   1
Meat   1

NUTRITION FACTS
Calories   287
Calories from Fat   101
Fat   11 g
  Saturated Fat   4 g
Cholesterol   53 mg
Sodium   654 mg*
Carbohydrate   27 g
  Dietary Fiber   1 g
  Sugars   4 g
Protein   20 g

3/4 lb	lean ground beef (85% lean)
1 can	(14 1/2 oz) SWANSON Vegetable Broth
1 Tbsp	Worcestershire sauce
1/2 tsp	dried oregano leaves, crushed
1/2 tsp	garlic powder
1 can	(about 8 oz) stewed tomatoes
1 1/2 cups	dry medium tube-shaped or corkscrew macaroni

1. In medium skillet over medium-high heat, cook beef until browned, stirring to separate meat. Pour off fat.
2. Add broth, Worcestershire, oregano, garlic powder, and tomatoes. Heat to a boil. Stir in macaroni. Reduce heat to low. Cover and cook 10 minutes, stirring often.
3. Uncover and cook 5 minutes more or until macaroni is done and most of liquid is absorbed. If desired, garnish with Parmesan cheese.

Number of Servings   4

* >400 mg of sodium

Recipe provided courtesy of Campbell Soup Company.

MEXICAN BEANS AND RICE

SERVING SIZE
1/5th recipe

EXCHANGES
PYRAMID SERVINGS
Starch   2 1/2

NUTRITION FACTS
Calories   195
Calories from Fat   12
Fat   1 g
  Saturated Fat   0 g
Cholesterol   1 mg
Sodium   436 mg*
Carbohydrate   38 g
  Dietary Fiber   4 g
  Sugars   3 g
Protein   8 g

1 can	(14 1/2 oz) SWANSON Chicken Broth
1/2 tsp	ground cumin
1/8 tsp	black pepper
1 medium	onion, chopped (about 1/2 cup)
1 small	green pepper, chopped (about 1/2 cup)
3/4 cup	uncooked long-grain rice
1 can	(about 15 oz) kidney beans, rinsed and drained

1. In medium saucepan, mix broth, cumin, black pepper, onion, and green pepper. Over medium-high heat, heat to a boil. Stir in rice. Reduce heat to low. Cover and cook 20 minutes or until rice is done and most of liquid is absorbed.
2. Add beans and heat through. If desired, garnish with lime, fresh cilantro, and red pepper.

Number of Servings   5

* >400 mg of sodium

Recipe provided courtesy of Campbell Soup Company.

Desserts and Breads

Tomato Soup Spice Cake
Apple Strudel
Blueberry-Peach Sundaes
Strawberry Angel Dessert
Corn Kernel Pancakes
Fresh Pear Sauce for Ice Cream
Two-Berry Cornmeal Muffin Tops
Fudge Ice Cream Sandwiches
Cherry Lattice Pie
Nectarine and Berry Pie
Strawberry Sauce
Orange Cream Cheese Glaze
Date Cake Squares
Fresh Plum Cobbler
Spiced Pumpkin Pie
Cinnamon Bread Pudding
Mile-High Apple Pie
Apricot-Almond Coffee Ring
Date Bran Muffins
Date-Nut Twist
Grandma's Noodle Kugel
Apple-Apricot Bars
Cream Cheese and Jelly Cookies
Blueberry Triangles
Chocolate-Cream Cheese Nuggets
Reduced-Fat Pie Pastry
Mom's Lemon Meringue Pie
Chewy Coconut Bars
Chocolate Cream Pie
Key Lime Pie
Banana Cream Pie

Sweet Potato Pie

Coconut Custard Pie

Summer Fruit Tart

Rich Chocolate Cheesecake

Granola Bites

Pineapple Upside-Down Cake

Banana Walnut Bread

Creamy Tapioca Pudding

Baked Vanilla Custard

Grandma's Apple Crisp

French Vanilla Freeze

Creamy Rice Pudding

Chocolate Crumb Pie

Little Lemon Cakes

Strawberry Pineapple Trifle

Peach Cobbler

Blueberry Muffins

Thumbprint Cookies

Fudgy Fructose Topping

Banana Bread

White Cake

Floating Islands With Fresh Fruit Sauce

Peach Parfait Pie

Apple Crisp Dessert

Multi-Grain Apple Raisin Muffins

Quickbread

Carob Treats

Fruit Crumble Cookies

Raisin Bran Applesauce Cookies

Granola Bars

Carrot Honey Oat Bran Muffins

Cinnamon Applesauce Bread

Applesauce Yogurt Delight

Chocolate Banana Split

Fresh Fruit Parfaits

Fruity Mousse

Lemon Souffle Cheesecake

Low Fat Blueberry Muffins

Sparkling Lemon Ice

White Chocolate Devil's Food Pie

Scalloped Apple Bake

Banana-Nana Split Pie

Southern Peachy Parfait

Igloo Cake

Eskimo Float

Angel Delight

TOMATO SOUP SPICE CAKE

SERVING SIZE
1/8th cake

EXCHANGES
Carbohydrate   4
Fat   2

PYRAMID SERVINGS
Starch   2
Sweet   2
Fat   2

NUTRITION FACTS
Calories   410
Calories from Fat   135
Fat   15 g
   Saturated Fat   4 g
Cholesterol   53 mg
Sodium   566 mg*
Carbohydrate   64 g
   Dietary Fiber   1 g
   Sugars   37 g
Protein   6 g

2 cups	all-purpose flour
1 1/3 cups	sugar
4 tsp	baking powder
1 1/2 tsp	ground allspice
1 tsp	baking soda
1 tsp	ground cinnamon
1/2 tsp	ground cloves
1 can	(10 3/4 oz) CAMPBELL'S condensed Tomato Soup
1/2 cup	vegetable shortening
2	eggs
1/4 cup	water
	Cream cheese frosting (optional)

1. Preheat oven to 350°F. Grease and flour two 8-inch round cake pans.
2. In large bowl, combine flour, sugar, baking powder, allspice, baking soda, cinnamon, cloves, soup, shortening, eggs, and water. With mixer at low speed, beat until well mixed, constantly scraping bowl with rubber spatula. At high speed, beat 4 minutes, occasionally scraping bowl. Pour batter into prepared pans.
3. Bake 35 to 40 minutes or until toothpick inserted in center comes out clean. Cool in pans on wire racks 10 minutes. Carefully remove from pans; cool completely. Frost with cream cheese frosting.
4. If desired, garnish with fresh mint and orange slices.

Number of Servings   8

* >400 mg of sodium

Recipe provided courtesy of Campbell Soup Company.

APPLE STRUDEL

SERVING SIZE
1/6th recipe

EXCHANGES
Carbohydrate   2 1/2
Fat   2

PYRAMID SERVINGS
Starch   1 1/2
Fruit   1
Fat   2

NUTRITION FACTS
Calories   259
Calories from Fat   101
Fat   11 g
   Saturated Fat   3 g
Cholesterol   35 mg
Sodium   136 mg
Carbohydrate   37 g
   Dietary Fiber   4 g
   Sugars   13 g
Protein   4 g

1 sheet	PEPPERIDGE FARM frozen Puff Pastry
1	egg
1 tsp	water
2 Tbsp	sugar
1 Tbsp	all-purpose flour
1/4 tsp	ground cinnamon
2 large	cooking apples, peeled, cored, and thinly sliced (about 3 cups)
2 Tbsp	raisins

1. Thaw pastry 20 minutes. In cup, combine egg and water; set aside. Meanwhile, pre-heat oven to 375°F. Grease 15 x 10-inch jelly-roll pan.
2. On lightly floured surface, roll out pastry sheet into a 15 x 12-in rectangle; place on prepared jelly-roll pan.
3. In large bowl, combine sugar, flour, and cinnamon. Add apples and raisins; toss to coat well. Arrange apple mixture down one 15-inch side of rectangle to within 1 inch of edge.
4. Brush edges of dough with some egg mixture. Roll up pastry, jelly-roll fashion, placing seam-side down on prepared pan. Pinch ends and tuck under. Brush strudel with egg mixture. Cut several 2-inch long diagonal slits, about 2 inches apart, on top of pastry. Bake 35 minutes or until golden.
5. Cool in pan on wire rack about 30 minutes before serving. Serve warm. If desired, garnish with whipped cream, cinnamon sticks, and fresh mint.

Number of Servings   6

Recipe provided courtesy of Campbell Soup Company.

BLUEBERRY-PEACH SUNDAES

SERVING SIZE
1/6th recipe (1/3 c
yogurt, 1/2 c fruit,
2 Tbsp topping)

EXCHANGES
Carbohydrate   2

PYRAMID SERVINGS
Fruit   1/2
Sweet   1 1/2

NUTRITION FACTS
Calories   172
Calories from Fat   3
Fat   0 g
   Saturated Fat   0 g
Cholesterol   0 mg
Sodium   100 mg
Carbohydrate   30 g
   Dietary Fiber   1 g
   Sugars   26 g
Protein   3 g

3/4 cup	MARIE'S Dessert Topping for Peaches
1/4 tsp	almond extract
2 cups	diced fresh nectarines or peaches (about 2 medium)
2 cups	vanilla nonfat frozen yogurt
1 cup	fresh blueberries

1. In small bowl, combine dessert topping and almond extract; set aside.
2. In 6 dessert dishes, spoon 1/3 cup yogurt. Divide nectarines and blueberries among dishes. Spoon 2 Tbsp dessert topping over fruit and yogurt. Serve immediately.

Number of Servings   6

Recipe provided courtesy of Campbell Soup Company.

141

STRAWBERRY ANGEL DESSERT

SERVING SIZE
1/12th recipe

EXCHANGES
Carbohydrate   3

PYRAMID SERVINGS
Sweet   3

NUTRITION FACTS
Calories   225
Calories from Fat   12
Fat   1 g
  Saturated Fat   1 g
Cholesterol   0 mg
Sodium   264 mg
Carbohydrate   40 g
  Dietary Fiber   2 g
  Sugars   31 g
Protein   3 g

1 pkg	(about 14 oz) angel food cake mix
4 cups	sliced fresh strawberries (about 1 qt)
1 jar	(14 oz) MARIE'S Dessert Topping for Strawberries
1 1/2 tsp	lemon juice
3/4 cup	thawed frozen whipped topping

1. Prepare cake according to package directions. Cool.
2. In bowl combine berries, dessert topping, and lemon juice.
3. With serrated knife, cut cake in half horizontally. Spoon two-thirds of berry mixture on bottom cake layer. Top with remaining layer; spoon remaining berry mixture on top. Serve with topping.

Number of Servings   12

CORN KERNEL PANCAKES

SERVING SIZE
1 pancake

EXCHANGES
PYRAMID SERVINGS
Starch   1

NUTRITION FACTS
Calories   76
Calories from Fat   2
Fat   0 g
    Saturated Fat   0 g
Cholesterol   0 mg
Sodium   150 mg
Carbohydrate   15 g
    Dietary Fiber   1 g
    Sugars   3 g
Protein   4 g

1 pkg	(10 oz) BIRD'S EYE frozen sweet corn, thawed
2/3 cup	all-purpose flour
2/3 cup	whole wheat flour
1 tsp	baking powder
1/2 tsp	baking soda
1/4 tsp	salt
1 cup	GUILT FREE nonfat sour cream
1/2 cup	GUILT FREE nonfat skim milk
2 large	egg whites
	Vegetable cooking spray

1. Combine all ingredients. Blend until smooth.
2. Spray large, nonstick skillet with vegetable cooking spray; heat over medium heat. Using a 1/4-cup measure, scoop batter onto hot skillet; spread into 3-inch rounds. Cook until tops are bubbling and bottom is browned; turn cakes over until underside is browned.
3. Serve pancakes warm with nonfat sour cream and/or unsweetened applesauce.

Number of Servings   15

FRESH PEAR SAUCE FOR ICE CREAM

SERVING SIZE
1/2 cup ice cream +
1/3 cup sauce

EXCHANGES
Carbohydrate   3

PYRAMID SERVINGS
Fruit   2
Milk   1/2
Sweet   1/2

NUTRITION FACTS
Calories   200
Calories from Fat   4
Fat   0 g
    Saturated Fat   0 g
Cholesterol   0 mg
Sodium   88 mg
Carbohydrate   49 g
    Dietary Fiber   2 g
    Sugars   34 g
Protein   4 g

2	firm Bartlett pears (about 1 1/4 lb)
3/4 cup	frozen white grape juice concentrate, thawed
1 Tbsp	lemon juice
1/2 tsp	almond extract
1 1/2 pt	GUILT FREE nonfat ice cream (Praline Pecan Crunch, Strawberry or Vanilla)
6 sprigs	fresh mint (optional)

1. Peel, quarter, core, and dice pears. Combine pears with thawed concentrate and lemon juice in medium saucepan. Bring to simmer. Cook uncovered, over medium-low heat until pears are soft, about 20 minutes.
2. Remove saucepan from heat; stir in almond extract. Pour into container to cool. Refrigerate until cold.
3. Scoop 1/2 cup (4 oz) ice cream into each dessert bowl or cup. Spoon 1/3 cup pear mixture over ice cream. Garnish with mint.

Number of Servings   6

TWO-BERRY CORNMEAL MUFFIN TOPS

SERVING SIZE
1 top

EXCHANGES
Starch   1 1/2

PYRAMID SERVINGS
Starch   1
Fruit   1/2

NUTRITION FACTS
Calories   116
Calories from Fat   2
Fat   0 g
    Saturated Fat   0 g
Cholesterol   0 mg
Sodium   162 mg
Carbohydrate   25 g
    Dietary Fiber   1 g
    Sugars   9 g
Protein   3 g

3/4 cup	all-purpose flour
3/4 cup	yellow cornmeal
1/2 tsp	baking powder
1/2 tsp	baking soda
1/4 tsp	salt
1/2 cup	GUILT FREE blueberry nonfat yogurt
1/2 cup	SMUCKER'S Simply Fruit seedless red raspberry spreadable fruit
2 large	egg whites
	Vegetable cooking spray

1. Heat oven to 375°F. Combine all dry ingredients in mixing bowl. Set aside.
2. Combine yogurt, spreadable fruit, and egg whites in small bowl. Beat with a fork. Add yogurt mixture to the flour mixture, stirring just until ingredients are well moistened. Do not overmix.
3. Using a 1/4-cup measure, scoop batter onto cookie sheet sprayed lightly with vegetable cooking spray. Space batter 2 1/2 inches apart. Bake until browned and firm to touch, about 15 minutes.

Number of Servings   **10**

FUDGE ICE CREAM SANDWICHES

SERVING SIZE
1 sandwich

EXCHANGES
Carbohydrate   3 1/2

PYRAMID SERVINGS
Starch   1
Fruit   1 1/2
Sweet   1

NUTRITION FACTS
Calories   213
Calories from Fat   9
Fat   1 g
    Saturated Fat   0 g
Cholesterol   0 mg
Sodium   220 mg
Carbohydrate   51 g
    Dietary Fiber   3 g
    Sugars   30 g
Protein   4 g

3/4 cup	unsweetened cocoa powder
1 tsp	ground cinnamon
1/2 tsp	baking soda
1/2 tsp	salt
1 can	(12 oz) frozen apple juice concentrate, thawed
1 cup	pitted prunes
1/2 cup	light corn syrup
1/2 cup	GUILT FREE nonfat sour cream
2 tsp	vanilla extract
1 cup	bleached all-purpose flour
	Nonstick vegetable spray
2 cups	GUILT FREE nonfat ice cream

1. Combine first four ingredients in medium mixing bowl. Stir. Add juice concentrate, whisk until smooth. Set aside.
2. Purée prunes and corn syrup. Add to cocoa mixture; whisk until blended. Add sour cream and vanilla; blend smooth. Add flour; whisk just until moistened. Do not overmix.
3. Heat oven to 350°F. Pour batter evenly onto 15 x 10-inch jelly-roll pan sprayed lightly with vegetable spray. Bake until center is firm, 15 to 20 minutes. Cool completely. Cut into 24 squares.
4. Soften ice cream in refrigerator for 15 minutes. Spoon 2 Tbsp ice cream onto each of 12 fudge squares. Assemble one by one, covering each with another fudge square to form sandwich. Place on tray in freezer. When sandwiches are firm, remove from freezer, wrap in plastic wrap. Return to freezer until ready to serve.

Number of Servings   12

CHERRY LATTICE PIE

SERVING SIZE
1/8th recipe

EXCHANGES
Carbohydrate 3 1/2
Fat 2

PYRAMID SERVINGS
Starch   2
Fruit   1
Sweet   1/2
Fat   2

NUTRITION FACTS
Calories   343
Calories from Fat   110
Fat   12 g
  Saturated Fat   2 g
Cholesterol   0 mg
Sodium   280 mg
Carbohydrate   50 g
  Dietary Fiber   2 g
  Sugars   15 g
Protein   5 g

2 pkg	(16 oz each) frozen no-sugar-added pitted cherries
12 3/4 tsp	EQUAL Measure or 42 packets EQUAL sweetener or 1 3/4 cup EQUAL Spoonful
4 tsp	flour
4 tsp	cornstarch
1/4 tsp	ground nutmeg
5–7 drops	red food color

1. Thaw cherries completely in strainer set in bowl; reserve 3/4 cup cherry juice. Mix EQUAL, flour, cornstarch, and nutmeg in small saucepan; stir in cherry juice and heat to boiling. Boil, stirring constantly, 1 minute. Remove from heat and stir in cherries; stir in food color.
2. Make pastry recipe on page 164.
3. Roll half the pastry on floured surface into circle 1 inch larger than inverted 9-inch pie pan; ease pastry into pan. Pour cherry mixture into pastry. Roll remaining pastry on floured surface to 1/8 inch thickness; cut into strips 1/2 inch wide. Arrange pastry strips on pie and weave into lattice design. Trim edge of pastry and strips and flute edge.
4. Bake in preheated 425°F oven until pastry is browned, 35 to 40 minutes. Cool on wire rack.

Number of Servings   8

NECTARINE AND BERRY PIE

SERVING SIZE
1/8th pie

EXCHANGES
Carbohydrate   2 1/2
Fat   1

PYRAMID SERVINGS
Starch   1 1/2
Fruit   1
Fat   1

NUTRITION FACTS
Calories   201
Calories from Fat   57
Fat   6 g
  Saturated Fat   1 g
Cholesterol   0 mg
Sodium   140 mg
Carbohydrate   34 g
  Dietary Fiber   3 g
  Sugars   12 g
Protein   3 g

	Reduced-Fat Pie Pastry (p. 164)
5 cups	sliced nectarines (about 5 medium)
1 cup	raspberries or sliced strawberries
1 cup	fresh or frozen blueberries, partially thawed
2 tsp	lemon juice
3 Tbsp	cornstarch
7 1/4 tsp	EQUAL Measure or 24 packets EQUAL sweetener or 1 cup EQUAL Spoonful
1 tsp	grated lemon rind
1/4 tsp	ground allspice

1. Roll pastry on floured surface into 12-inch circle; transfer to ungreased cookie sheet.
2. Toss nectarines and berries with lemon juice in large bowl; sprinkle fruit with combined cornstarch, EQUAL, lemon rind, and allspice and toss. Arrange fruit on pastry. Bring edges of pastry to center, overlapping as necessary. Bake pie in preheated 425°F oven until pastry is golden and fruit is tender, 35 to 40 minutes. Cool on wire rack.

Number of Servings   8

STRAWBERRY SAUCE

SERVING SIZE
2 Tbsp

EXCHANGES
PYRAMID SERVINGS
Free Food

NUTRITION FACTS
Calories   12
Calories from Fat   0
Fat   0 g
   Saturated Fat   0 g
Cholesterol   0 mg
Sodium   1 mg
Carbohydrate   3 g
   Dietary Fiber   1 g
   Sugars   2 g
Protein   0 g

1 pkg	(16 oz) frozen unsweetened strawberries, thawed
1 Tbsp	lemon juice
1 3/4 tsp	EQUAL Measure or 6 packets EQUAL sweetener or 1/4 cup EQUAL Spoonful

Process strawberries in food processor or blender until smooth. Stir in lemon juice and EQUAL; refrigerate until serving time.

Makes about 2 cups
Number of Servings   16

ORANGE CREAM CHEESE GLAZE

SERVING SIZE
1 1/2 tsp

EXCHANGES
PYRAMID SERVINGS
Free Food

NUTRITION FACTS
Calories   19
Calories from Fat   14
Fat   2 g
   Saturated Fat   1 g
Cholesterol   5 mg
Sodium   31 mg
Carbohydrate   1 g
   Dietary Fiber   0 g
   Sugars   1 g
Protein   1 g

1/2 pkg	(8 oz) reduced-fat cream cheese, softened
1/2–1 tsp	orange extract
1 tsp	EQUAL Measure or 3 packets EQUAL sweetener or 2 Tbsp EQUAL Spoonful
	Skim milk

Mix cream cheese, extract, EQUAL, and enough milk to make medium glaze consistency.

Makes about 1/2 cup
Number of Servings   16

DATE CAKE SQUARES

SERVING SIZE
1 square

EXCHANGES
Carbohydrate   1
Fat   1

PYRAMID SERVINGS
Starch   1/2
Fruit   1/2
Fat   1

NUTRITION FACTS
Calories   111
Calories from Fat   46
Fat   5 g
   Saturated Fat   1 g
Cholesterol   18 mg
Sodium   127 mg
Carbohydrate   16 g
   Dietary Fiber   1 g
   Sugars   10 g
Protein   2 g

1 cup	chopped dates
3/4 cup	chopped pitted prunes
1/2 cup	dark raisins
1 1/4 cups	water
8 Tbsp	margarine, cut into pieces
2	eggs
1 tsp	vanilla
1 cup	all-purpose flour
5 1/2 tsp	EQUAL Measure or 18 packets EQUAL sweetener or 3/4 cup EQUAL Spoonful
1 tsp	baking soda
1/4 tsp	salt
1/2 tsp	ground cinnamon
1/4 tsp	ground nutmeg
1/4 cup	chopped walnuts

1. Combine dates, prunes, raisins, and water in medium saucepan; heat to boiling. Reduce heat and simmer, uncovered, until fruit is tender and water is absorbed, about 10 minutes. Remove from heat and add margarine, stirring until melted; cool.
2. Mix eggs and vanilla into fruit mixture. Mix combined flour, EQUAL, baking soda, salt, cinnamon, and nutmeg and add to mixture. Spread batter evenly in greased baking dish, 11 x 7 x 2-inch; sprinkle with walnuts.
3. Bake in preheated 350°F oven until cake springs back when touched lightly, 30 to 35 minutes. Cool on wire rack; cut into 24 squares.

Number of Servings   24

FRESH PLUM COBBLER

SERVING SIZE
1/6th recipe

EXCHANGES
Carbohydrate   2 1/2
Fat   1

PYRAMID SERVINGS
Starch   1 1/2
Fruit   1
Fat   1

NUTRITION FACTS
Calories   229
Calories from Fat   60
Fat   7 g
  Saturated Fat   1 g
Cholesterol   0 mg
Sodium   362 mg
Carbohydrate   40 g
  Dietary Fiber   2 g
  Sugars   15 g
Protein   4 g

1/2 cup	water
5 1/2 tsp	EQUAL Measure or 18 packets EQUAL sweetener or 3/4 cup EQUAL Spoonful
1 1/2 Tbsp	cornstarch
1 tsp	lemon juice
4 cups	sliced pitted plums
1/4 tsp	ground nutmeg
1/8 tsp	ground allspice
1 cup	all-purpose flour
1 1/2 tsp	baking powder
1 3/4 tsp	EQUAL Measure or 6 packets EQUAL sweetener or 1/4 cup EQUAL Spoonful
1/2 tsp	salt
1/8 tsp	ground allspice
3 Tbsp	cold margarine, cut into pieces
1/2 cup	skim milk

1. Combine water, 5 1/2 tsp EQUAL, corn-starch, and lemon juice in large saucepan; add plums and heat to boiling. Boil, stirring constantly, until thickened, about 1 minute. Stir in nutmeg and 1/8 tsp allspice. Pour mixture into ungreased 1 1/2-qt casserole.
2. Combine flour, baking powder, remaining EQUAL, salt, and 1/8 tsp allspice in medium bowl; cut in margarine with pastry blender until mixture resembles coarse crumbs. Stir in milk, forming dough. Spoon dough into 6 mounds on fruit.
3. Bake cobbler, uncovered, in preheated 400°F oven until topping is golden brown, about 25 minutes. Serve warm.

Number of Servings   6

SPICED PUMPKIN PIE

SERVING SIZE
1/8th pie

EXCHANGES
Carbohydrate   2
Fat   1 1/2

PYRAMID SERVINGS
Starch   2
Fat   1 1/2

NUTRITION FACTS
Calories   222
Calories from Fat   72
Fat   8 g
  Saturated Fat   2 g
Cholesterol   81 mg
Sodium   294 mg
Carbohydrate   29 g
  Dietary Fiber   2 g
  Sugars   10 g
Protein   9 g

	Reduced-Fat Pie Pastry (p. 164)
1 can	(16 oz) pumpkin
1 can	(12 oz) evaporated skim milk
3	eggs
5 1/2 tsp	EQUAL Measure or 18 packets EQUAL sweetener or 3/4 cup EQUAL Spoonful
1/4 tsp	salt
1 tsp	ground cinnamon
1/2 tsp	ground ginger
1/4 tsp	ground nutmeg
1/8 tsp	ground cloves

1. Roll pastry on floured surface to circle 1 inch larger than inverted pie pan. Ease pastry into pan; trim and flute edge.
2. Beat pumpkin, evaporated milk, and eggs in medium bowl; beat in remaining ingredients. Pour mixture into pastry shell. Bake in preheated 425°F oven 15 minutes; reduce heat to 350°F and bake until knife inserted near center comes out clean, about 40 minutes. Cool on wire rack.

Number of Servings   8

CINNAMON BREAD PUDDING

SERVING SIZE
1/8th recipe

EXCHANGES
Carbohydrate   1 1/2
Fat   1

PYRAMID SERVINGS
Starch   1 1/2
Fat   1

NUTRITION FACTS
Calories   177
Calories from Fat   68
Fat   8 g
   Saturated Fat   1 g
Cholesterol   28 mg
Sodium   360 mg
Carbohydrate   20 g
   Dietary Fiber   1 g
   Sugars   6 g
Protein   6 g

2 cups	skim milk
4 Tbsp	margarine, cut into pieces
1	egg
2	egg whites
3 1/2 tsp	EQUAL Measure, or 12 packets EQUAL sweetener or 1/2 cup EQUAL Spoonful
1 1/2 tsp	ground cinnamon
1/8 tsp	ground cloves
3 dashes	ground mace
1/4 tsp	salt
6 cups	cubed day-old French or Italian bread (3/4-inch cubes)

1. Heat milk and margarine to simmering in medium saucepan; remove from heat and stir until margarine is melted. Cool 10 minutes.
2. Beat egg and egg whites in large bowl until foamy; mix in EQUAL; spices, and salt. Mix milk mixture into egg mixture; mix in bread.
3. Spoon mixture into ungreased 1 1/2-qt casserole. Place casserole in roasting pan on oven rack; add 1 inch hot water. Bake, uncovered, in preheated 350°F oven until pudding is set and sharp knife inserted halfway between center and edge comes out clean, 40 to 45 minutes.

Number of Servings   8

MILE-HIGH APPLE PIE

SERVING SIZE
1/8th recipe

EXCHANGES
Carbohydrate   4
Fat   2

PYRAMID SERVINGS
Starch   2 1/2
Fruit   1 1/2
Fat   2

NUTRITION FACTS
Calories   358
Calories from Fat   110
Fat   12 g
    Saturated Fat   2 g
Cholesterol   0 mg
Sodium   352 mg
Carbohydrate   59 g
    Dietary Fiber   4 g
    Sugars   24 g
Protein   4 g

	Reduced-Fat Pie Pastry (for double-crust pie) (p. 164)
3 Tbsp	cornstarch
7 1/4 tsp	EQUAL Measure or 24 packets EQUAL sweetener or 1 cup EQUAL Spoonful
3/4 tsp	ground cinnamon
1/4 tsp	ground nutmeg
1/4 tsp	salt
8 cups	sliced cored peeled Granny Smith or other baking apples (about 8 medium)

1. Roll half the pastry on floured surface into circle 1 inch larger than inverted pie pan. Ease pastry into pan.
2. Combine cornstarch, EQUAL, cinnamon, nutmeg, and salt; sprinkle over apples in large bowl and toss. Arrange apples in pie crust.
3. Roll remaining pastry into circle large enough to fit top of pie. Cut hearts in pastry with cutters; place pastry on pie, seal edges, trim, and flute. Press pastry hearts on pastry. Bake in preheated 425°F oven until pastry is golden and apples are tender, 40 to 50 minutes. Cool on wire rack.

Number of Servings   8

APRICOT-ALMOND COFFEE RING

SERVING SIZE
1/12th recipe

EXCHANGES
Starch   2

PYRAMID SERVINGS
Starch   1 1/2
Fruit   1/2

NUTRITION FACTS
Calories   153
Calories from Fat   27
Fat   3 g
  Saturated Fat   0 g
Cholesterol   0 mg
Sodium   222 mg
Carbohydrate   28 g
  Dietary Fiber   3 g
  Sugars   7 g
Protein   4 g

1 cup	dried apricots, sliced
1 cup	water
3 1/2 tsp	EQUAL Measure or 12 packets EQUAL sweetener or 1/2 cup EQUAL Spoonful
1/8 tsp	ground mace
1 loaf	(16 oz) frozen Italian bread dough, thawed
1/3 cup	sliced or slivered almonds Skim milk
1 tsp	EQUAL Measure or 3 packets EQUAL sweetener or 2 Tbsp EQUAL Spoonful

1. Heat apricots, water, 3 1/2 tsp EQUAL, and mace to boiling in small saucepan; reduce heat and simmer, covered, until apricots are tender and water is absorbed, about 10 minutes. Simmer, uncovered, until no water remains, 2 to 3 minutes. Cool.
2. Roll dough on floured surface into 14 x 8-inch rectangle. Spread apricot mixture on dough to within 1 inch of the edges; sprinkle with 1/4 cup almonds. Roll dough up, beginning with long edge; pinch edge of dough to seal. Place dough seam-side down on greased cookie sheet, forming circle; pinch ends to seal.
3. Using scissors, cut dough from outside edge almost to center, making cuts 1 inch apart. Turn each section cut-side up so that filling shows. Let rise, covered, in warm place until dough is double in size, about 1 hour.
4. Brush top of dough lightly with milk and sprinkle with remaining almonds and 1 tsp EQUAL. Bake coffee cake in preheated 375°F oven until golden, 25 to 30 minutes. Cool on wire rack.

Number of Servings   **12**

DATE BRAN MUFFINS

SERVING SIZE
1 muffin

EXCHANGES
PYRAMID SERVINGS
Starch   1 1/2
Fat   1

NUTRITION FACTS
Calories   156
Calories from Fat   52
Fat   6 g
    Saturated Fat   1 g
Cholesterol   18 mg
Sodium   323 mg
Carbohydrate   23 g
    Dietary Fiber   2 g
    Sugars   8 g
Protein   4 g

1 1/2 cups	wheat bran cereal
1 1/2 cups	skim milk
1/3 cup	margarine, melted
1	egg
1 tsp	vanilla
1 1/4 cups	all-purpose flour
4 1/4 tsp	EQUAL Measure or 14 packets EQUAL sweetener or 1/2 cup + 2 Tbsp EQUAL Spoonful
1 Tbsp	baking powder
1/2 tsp	salt
2 tsp	ground cinnamon
1/2 cup	pitted dates, chopped

1. Combine cereal and milk in medium bowl; let stand 5 minutes. Stir in margarine, egg, and vanilla. Add combined flour, EQUAL, baking powder, salt, and cinnamon, stirring just until mixture is blended. Stir in dates.
2. Spoon batter into greased muffin tins; bake in preheated 375°F oven until muffins are browned and toothpicks inserted in centers come out clean, 20 to 25 minutes. Cool in pans on wire rack 5 minutes; remove from pans and cool on wire racks.

Number of Servings   12

DATE-NUT TWIST

SERVING SIZE
1/16th recipe

EXCHANGES
Starch   1 1/2
Polyunsat Fat   1/2

PYRAMID SERVINGS
Sweet   1 1/2
Fat   1/2

NUTRITION FACTS
Calories   129
Calories from Fat   30
Fat   3 g
  Saturated Fat   0 g
Cholesterol   0 mg
Sodium   175 mg
Carbohydrate   22 g
  Dietary Fiber   2 g
  Sugars   7 g
Protein   4 g

3/4 cup	pitted dates, chopped
1/2 cup	coarsely chopped walnuts
2	egg whites
3 1/2 tsp	EQUAL Measure or 12 packets EQUAL sweetener or 1/2 cup EQUAL Spoonful
2 tsp	grated lemon rind
1 loaf	(16 oz) frozen Italian bread dough, thawed
1	egg white
2 tsp	water
1 tsp	EQUAL Measure or 3 packets EQUAL sweetener or 2 Tbsp EQUAL Spoonful

1. Combine dates, 1/4 cup walnuts, egg whites, 3 1/2 tsp EQUAL Measure, and lemon rind in small bowl.
2. Roll dough on floured surface into rectangle 20 x 6 inches. Spread date mixture on dough to within 1 inch of edges. Roll dough up, beginning with long edge; pinch edge of dough to seal. Cut roll into 2 equal pieces. Place rolls on greased cookie sheet and twist together, tucking ends under. Let rise, covered, in warm place until dough is double in size, about 1 hour.
3. Beat egg white and water in small bowl; brush over top of dough. Sprinkle dough with remaining EQUAL and remaining 1/4 cup walnuts. Bake in preheated 375°F oven until golden, about 35 minutes. Cool on wire rack.

Number of Servings   16

GRANDMA'S NOODLE KUGEL

SERVING SIZE
1/12th recipe

EXCHANGES
Carbohydrate   2 1/2
Fat   1 1/2

PYRAMID SERVINGS
Starch   1 1/2
Fruit   1
Fat   1 1/2

NUTRITION FACTS
Calories   253
Calories from Fat   67
Fat   7 g
    Saturated Fat   3 g
Cholesterol   62 mg
Sodium   199 mg
Carbohydrate   36 g
    Dietary Fiber   2 g
    Sugars   15 g
Protein   11 g

1/4 cup	margarine, softened
3	eggs
1 1/2 cups	reduced-fat cottage cheese
1 cup	reduced-fat sour cream
1 can	(20 oz) crushed pineapple in juice, drained
1/2 cup	dark raisins
1/2 tsp	ground cinnamon
5 1/2 tsp	EQUAL Measure or 18 packets EQUAL sweetener or 3/4 cup EQUAL Spoonful
1 pkg	(12 oz) cholesterol-free wide noodles, cooked

1. Mix margarine and eggs in large bowl until smooth; mix in cottage cheese, sour cream, pineapple, raisins, cinnamon, and EQUAL. Mix in noodles.
2. Spoon mixture evenly into lightly greased 13 x 9 x 2-inch baking dish. Bake kugel in preheated 325°F oven, uncovered, until heated through, 45 to 55 minutes. Cut into squares.

Number of Servings   12

APPLE-APRICOT BARS

SERVING SIZE
1 bar

EXCHANGES
Carbohydrate   1/2
Fat   1/2

PYRAMID SERVINGS
Starch   1/2
Fat   1/2

NUTRITION FACTS
Calories   60
Calories from Fat   18
Fat   2 g
    Saturated Fat   0 g
Cholesterol   7 mg
Sodium   67 mg
Carbohydrate   9 g
    Dietary Fiber   1 g
    Sugars   3 g
Protein   1 g

3/4 cup	chopped dried apples
3/4 cup	chopped dried apricots
3 1/2 tsp	EQUAL Measure or 12 packets EQUAL sweetener or 1/2 cup EQUAL Spoonful
1 cup	water
5 Tbsp	margarine, softened
1 3/4 tsp	EQUAL Measure or 6 packets EQUAL sweetener or 1/4 cup EQUAL Spoonful
1	egg
2	egg whites
1 tsp	vanilla
1 3/4 cups	all-purpose flour
1/2 tsp	baking soda
1/4 tsp	salt
	Skim milk

1. Heat apples, apricots, 3 1/2 tsp EQUAL, and water to boiling in small saucepan; reduce heat and simmer, uncovered, until fruit is tender and water is absorbed, about 10 minutes. Process mixture in food processor or blender until smooth; cool.
2. Beat margarine and 1 3/4 tsp EQUAL in medium bowl until fluffy; beat in egg, egg whites, and vanilla. Mix in combined flour, baking soda, and salt. Divide dough into 4 equal parts; roll each into a log about 5 inches long. Refrigerate, covered, until firm, about 2 hours.
3. Roll 1 piece dough on floured surface into rectangle 12 x 4 inches. Spread 1/4 of the fruit filling in a 1 1/2-inch strip in the center of dough. Fold sides of dough over filling, pressing edges to seal. Cut filled dough in half and place on greased cookie sheet. Repeat with remaining dough and fruit filling.
4. Brush top of dough lightly with milk; bake in preheated 400°F oven until lightly browned, 10 to 12 minutes. Remove from pan and cool on wire racks; cut into 1 1/2-inch bars. Store in airtight container.

CREAM CHEESE AND JELLY COOKIES

SERVING SIZE
1 cookie

EXCHANGES
Carbohydrate   1/2
Fat   1

PYRAMID SERVINGS
Starch   1/2
Fat   1

NUTRITION FACTS
Calories   81
Calories from Fat   47
Fat   5 g
  Saturated Fat   2 g
Cholesterol   4 mg
Sodium   86 mg
Carbohydrate   7 g
  Dietary Fiber   0 g
  Sugars   2 g
Protein   1 g

3/4 cup	margarine, softened
1 pkg	(8 oz) reduced-fat cream cheese, softened
2 1/2 tsp	EQUAL Measure or 8 packets EQUAL sweetener or 1/3 cup EQUAL Spoonful
2 cups	all-purpose flour
1/4 tsp	salt
1/4 cup	black cherry or seedless raspberry spreadable fruit

1. Beat margarine, cream cheese, and EQUAL in medium bowl until fluffy; mix in flour and salt, forming a soft dough. Refrigerate, covered, until dough is firm, about 3 hours.
2. Roll dough on lightly floured surface into circle 1/8 inch thick; cut into rounds with 3-inch cutter. Place rounded 1/4 tsp spreadable fruit in center of each round; fold rounds into halves and crimp edges firmly with tines of fork. Pierce tops of cookies with tip of sharp knife.
3. Bake cookies on greased cookie sheets in preheated 350°F oven until lightly browned, about 10 minutes. Cool on wire racks.

Number of Servings   36

BLUEBERRY TRIANGLES

SERVING SIZE
1 triangle

EXCHANGES
Carbohydrate   1 1/2
Fat   1

PYRAMID SERVINGS
Starch   1
Fruit   1/2
Fat   1

NUTRITION FACTS
Calories   152
Calories from Fat   54
Fat   6 g
  Saturated Fat   1 g
Cholesterol   0 mg
Sodium   143 mg
Carbohydrate   22 g
  Dietary Fiber   1 g
  Sugars   5 g
Protein   2 g

1 1/2 cups	fresh or frozen blueberries, slightly thawed
3 1/2 tsp	EQUAL Measure or 12 packets EQUAL sweetener or 1/2 cup EQUAL Spoonful
1 1/2 tsp	cornstarch
2–4 tsp	cold water
	Pastry for 9-inch pie (p. 164)
	Skim milk
1/2 tsp	EQUAL Measure or 1 1/2 packets EQUAL sweetener or 1 Tbsp EQUAL Spoonful

1. Rinse blueberries; drain slightly and place in medium saucepan. Sprinkle berries with 3 1/2 tsp EQUAL and cornstarch and toss. Cook berries over medium heat, stirring constantly. Add water, 1 tsp at a time, if bottom of saucepan becomes dry, cooking and stirring until berries begin to release juice and form a small amount of thickened sauce. Cool; refrigerate until chilled.
2. Roll pastry on floured surface to 1/8 inch thickness; cut into 8 squares, 5 x 5 inches, rerolling scraps as necessary. Place scant 2 Tbsp blueberry mixture on each pastry square; fold in half to form triangles and press edges together. Flute edges of pastry or crimp with tines of fork; pierce tops of pastries 3 or 4 times with tip of knife.
3. Brush tops of pastries lightly with milk and sprinkle with 1/2 tsp EQUAL. Bake on foil or parchment-lined cookie sheet in preheated 400°F oven until pastries are browned, about 25 minutes.

Number of Servings   8

CHOCOLATE-CREAM CHEESE NUGGETS

SERVING SIZE
1 nugget

EXCHANGES
Carbohydrate 1/2
Fat 1/2

PYRAMID SERVINGS
Starch 1/2
Fat 1/2

NUTRITION FACTS
Calories 56
Calories from Fat 28
Fat 3 g
  Saturated Fat 1 g
Cholesterol 8 mg
Sodium 99 mg
Carbohydrate 6 g
  Dietary Fiber 0 g
  Sugars 3 g
Protein 1 g

1 cup	pitted prunes, chopped
1 cup	water
1/2 cup	margarine, softened
3 Tbsp	EQUAL Measure or 30 packets EQUAL sweetener or 1 1/4 cup EQUAL Spoonful
1	egg
1 1/3 cups	all-purpose flour
1/3 cup	Dutch or European processed cocoa
1 1/4 tsp	baking soda
1/2 tsp	salt
1 tsp	ground allspice
1 pkg	(8 oz) reduced-fat cream cheese, softened
1 3/4 tsp	EQUAL Measure or 6 packets EQUAL sweetener or 1/4 cup EQUAL Spoonful

1. Combine prunes and water in medium saucepan; heat to boiling. Reduce heat and simmer, uncovered, until prunes are very soft and water is absorbed, stirring occasionally. Cool to room temperature. Process prunes in food processor or blender until smooth.
2. Beat margarine and 3 Tbsp EQUAL in large bowl until fluffy; beat in prune mixture and egg. Mix in combined flour, cocoa, baking soda, salt, and allspice. Spoon dough by rounded tsp into greased mini-muffin cups. (Mixture will be very stiff.)
3. Beat cream cheese and 1 3/4 tsp EQUAL in small bowl until fluffy. Top dough in muffin cups with rounded 1/2 tsp cheese mixture; swirl into chocolate mixture with tip of knife. Bake cookies in preheated 350°F oven until lightly browned on the bottoms, about 12 minutes. Cool cookies in pans on wire racks 2 to 3 minutes; remove from pans and cool on wire racks.

Number of Servings **48**

REDUCED-FAT PIE PASTRY

SERVING SIZE
1/8th pie

EXCHANGES
PYRAMID SERVINGS
Starch   1
Fat   1

NUTRITION FACTS
Calories   125
Calories from Fat   53
Fat   6 g
  Saturated Fat   1 g
Cholesterol   0 mg
Sodium   140 mg
Carbohydrate   16 g
  Dietary Fiber   1 g
  Sugars   1 g
Protein   2 g

1 1/4 cups	all-purpose flour
1 tsp	EQUAL Measure or 3 packets EQUAL sweetener or 2 Tbsp EQUAL Spoonful
1/4 tsp	salt
4 Tbsp	cold margarine, cut into pieces
5–5 1/2 Tbsp	ice water

Combine flour, EQUAL, and salt in medium bowl; cut in margarine with pastry blender until mixture resembles coarse crumbs. Mix in water, 1 Tbsp at a time, mixing lightly with a fork after each addition until a dough is formed. Refrigerate until ready to use.

Tip: Double recipe for double-crust or lattice pies.

Makes pastry for 9-inch pie
Number of Servings   8

MOM'S LEMON MERINGUE PIE

SERVING SIZE
1/8th recipe

EXCHANGES
Carbohydrate   2
Fat   1 1/2

PYRAMID SERVINGS
Starch   1 1/2
Sweet   1/2
Fat   1 1/2

NUTRITION FACTS
Calories   240
Calories from Fat   90
Fat   10 g
    Saturated Fat   2 g
Cholesterol   53 mg
Sodium   227 mg
Carbohydrate   31 g
    Dietary Fiber   1 g
    Sugars   8 g
Protein   6 g

	Reduced-Fat Pie Pastry (p. 164)
2 1/4 cups	water
1/2 cup	lemon juice
10 3/4 tsp	EQUAL Measure or 36 packets EQUAL sweetener or 1 1/2 cups EQUAL Spoonful
1/3 cup	plus 2 Tbsp cornstarch
2	eggs
2	egg whites
1 tsp	finely grated lemon peel (optional)
2 Tbsp	margarine
1–2 drops	yellow food color (optional)
3	egg whites
1/4 tsp	cream of tartar
3 1/2 tsp	EQUAL Measure or 12 packets EQUAL sweetener (EQUAL Spoonful cannot be used in meringue recipes)

1. Roll pastry on lightly floured surface into circle 1 inch larger than inverted 9-inch pie pan. Ease pastry into pan; trim and flute edge. Pierce bottom and side of pastry with fork. Bake in preheated 425°F oven until pastry is browned, 10 to 15 minutes. Cool on wire rack.
2. Mix water, lemon juice, 10 3/4 tsp EQUAL (or other EQUAL products) and cornstarch in medium saucepan. Heat to boiling over medium-high heat, stirring constantly with a wire whisk. Boil and stir 1 minute; remove from heat. Beat eggs and 2 egg whites in small bowl; stir in about half of hot cornstarch mixture. Stir egg mixture back into remaining cornstarch mixture in

Continued

MOM'S LEMON MERINGUE PIE *Continued*

saucepan; cook and stir over low heat 1 minute. Remove from heat, add margarine, stirring until melted. Stir in food color, if desired. Pour mixture into baked pie shell.

3. Beat 3 egg whites in medium bowl with electric mixer until foamy; add cream of tartar and beat to soft peaks. Gradually beat in 3 1/2 tsp EQUAL or 12 packets EQUAL sweetener, beating until stiff peaks form. Spread meringue over hot lemon filling, carefully sealing to edge of crust to prevent shrinking or weeping.

4. Bake pie in preheated 425°F oven until meringue is lightly browned, about 5 minutes. Cool completely on wire rack before cutting.

Number of Servings   8

CHEWY COCONUT BARS

SERVING SIZE
1 bar

EXCHANGES
Carbohydrate   1/2
Fat   2

PYRAMID SERVINGS
Starch   1/2
Fat   2

NUTRITION FACTS
Calories   127
Calories from Fat   85
Fat   9 g
  Saturated Fat   4 g
Cholesterol   27 mg
Sodium   136 mg
Carbohydrate   10 g
  Dietary Fiber   1 g
  Sugars   5 g
Protein   2 g

2	eggs
7 1/4 tsp	EQUAL Measure or 24 packets EQUAL sweetener or 1 cup EQUAL Spoonful
1/4 tsp	maple flavoring
1/2 cup	margarine, melted
1 tsp	vanilla
1/2 cup	all-purpose flour
1 tsp	baking powder
1/4 tsp	salt
1 cup	unsweetened coconut,* finely chopped
1/2 cup	chopped walnuts (optional)†
1/2 cup	raisins

1. Beat eggs, EQUAL, and maple flavoring in medium bowl; mix in margarine and vanilla. Combine flour, baking powder, and salt in small bowl; stir into egg mixture. Mix in coconut, walnuts, and raisins. Spread batter evenly in greased 8-inch square baking pan.
2. Bake in preheated 350°F oven until browned and toothpick inserted in center comes out clean, about 20 minutes. Cool in pan on wire rack; cut into squares.

Number of Servings   16

*Unsweetened coconut can be purchased at health food stores. Or, substitute sweetened coconut and decrease the amount of EQUAL to 5 1/4 tsp EQUAL Measure or 18 packets of EQUAL sweetener or 3/4 cup EQUAL Spoonful.
†Walnuts not included in nutrient analysis.

CHOCOLATE CREAM PIE

SERVING SIZE
1/8th recipe

EXCHANGES
Carbohydrate   2 1/2
Fat   1

PYRAMID SERVINGS
Starch   1 1/2
Milk   1/2
Sweet   1/2

NUTRITION FACTS
Calories   239
Calories from Fat   74
Fat   8 g
  Saturated Fat   2 g
Cholesterol   55 mg
Sodium   253 mg
Carbohydrate   33 g
  Dietary Fiber   1 g
  Sugars   11 g
Protein   8 g

	Reduced-Fat Pie Pastry (p. 164)
1/3 cup	cornstarch
1/4–1/3 cup	European or Dutch processed cocoa
10 3/4 tsp	EQUAL Measure or 36 packets EQUAL sweetener or 1 1/2 cups EQUAL Spoonful
1/8 tsp	salt
3 cups	skim milk
2	eggs
2	egg whites
1 tsp	vanilla
8 Tbsp	thawed frozen light whipped topping

1. Roll pastry on lightly floured surface into circle 1 inch larger than inverted 9-inch pie pan. Ease pastry into pan; trim and flute edge. Pierce bottom and side of pastry with fork. Bake in preheated 425°F oven until crust is browned, 10 to 15 minutes. Cool on wire rack.
2. Combine cornstarch, cocoa, EQUAL, and salt in medium saucepan; stir in milk. Heat to boiling over medium-high heat, whisking constantly. Boil until thickened, about 1 minute.
3. Beat eggs and egg whites in small bowl; whisk about 1 cup chocolate mixture into eggs. Whisk egg mixture into chocolate mixture in saucepan. Cook over very low heat, whisking constantly, 30 to 60 seconds. Remove from heat; stir in vanilla.
4. Spread hot filling in baked crust; refrigerate until chilled and set, about 6 hours. Cut into wedges and place on serving plates. Garnish each serving with dollop of whipped topping and chocolate leaves, if desired.

Number of Servings   8

KEY LIME PIE

SERVING SIZE
1/8th recipe

EXCHANGES
Carbohydrate   1
Fat   2 1/2

PYRAMID SERVINGS
Starch   1/2
Sweet   1/2
Fat   2 1/2

NUTRITION FACTS
Calories   191
Calories from Fat   104
Fat   11 g
  Saturated Fat   5 g
Cholesterol   21 mg
Sodium   258 mg
Carbohydrate   16 g
  Dietary Fiber   0 g
  Sugars   8 g
Protein   6 g

1 cup	graham cracker crumbs
3 Tbsp	melted margarine
1 tsp	EQUAL Measure or 3 packets EQUAL sweetener or 2 Tbsp EQUAL Spoonful
1 envelope	(1/4 oz) unflavored gelatin
1 3/4 cups	skim milk
1 pkg	(8 oz) reduced-fat cream cheese, softened
1/3 to 1/2 cup	fresh lime juice
3 1/2 tsp	EQUAL Measure or 12 packets EQUAL sweetener or 1/2 cup EQUAL Spoonful
	Lime slices, raspberries, and fresh mint sprigs, for garnish (optional)

1. Combine graham cracker crumbs, margarine and 1 tsp EQUAL Measure or 3 packets EQUAL sweetener or 2 Tbsp EQUAL Spoonful in bottom of 7-inch springform pan; pat evenly on bottom and 1/2 inch up side of pan.
2. Sprinkle gelatin over 1/2 cup milk in small saucepan; let stand 2 to 3 minutes. Cook over low heat, stirring constantly, until gelatin is dissolved. Beat cream cheese in small bowl until fluffy; beat in remaining 1 1/4 cups milk and gelatin mixture. Mix in lime juice and 3 1/2 tsp EQUAL Measure or 12 packets EQUAL sweetener or 1/2 cup EQUAL Spoonful. Refrigerate pie until set, about 2 hours.
3. To serve, loosen side of pie from pan with small spatula and remove side of pan. Place pie on serving plate; garnish with lime slices, raspberries, and mint, if desired.

Number of Servings   8

BANANA CREAM PIE

SERVING SIZE
1/8th pie

EXCHANGES
Carbohydrate   2
Fat   1 1/2

PYRAMID SERVINGS
Starch   1
Fruit   1/2
Fat   1 1/2
Sweet   1/2

NUTRITION FACTS
Calories   214
Calories from Fat   67
Fat   7 g
  Saturated Fat   2 g
Cholesterol   55 mg
Sodium   237 mg
Carbohydrate   30 g
  Dietary Fiber   1 g
  Sugars   12 g
Protein   7 g

	Reduced-Fat Pie Pastry (p. 164)
1/3 cup	cornstarch
3 1/2 tsp	EQUAL Measure or 12 packets EQUAL sweetener or 1/2 cup EQUAL Spoonful
1/8 tsp	salt
2 1/2 cups	skim milk
2	egg yolks
1 tsp	vanilla
2	bananas, sliced
3	egg whites
1/4 tsp	cream of tartar
3 1/2 tsp	EQUAL Measure or 12 packets EQUAL sweetener

1. Roll pastry on lightly floured surface into circle 1 inch larger than inverted 9-inch pie pan. Ease pastry into pan; trim and flute edge. Pierce bottom and side of pastry with fork. Bake in preheated 425°F oven until crust is browned, 10 to 15 minutes. Cool on wire rack.
2. Combine cornstarch, 3 1/2 tsp EQUAL Measure or 12 packets EQUAL sweetener or 1/2 cup EQUAL Spoonful and salt in medium saucepan; stir in milk. Heat to boiling over medium-high heat, whisking constantly. Boil until thickened, about 1 minute, whisking constantly.
3. Beat egg yolks and vanilla in small bowl; whisk about 1 cup hot custard mixture into eggs. Whisk egg mixture back into custard mixture in saucepan. Cook over very low heat, whisking constantly, 30 to 60 seconds. Arrange bananas in bottom of baked crust; pour custard mixture over bananas, spreading evenly.

Continued

BANANA CREAM PIE *Continued*

4. Beat egg whites in medium bowl with electric mixer until foamy; add cream of tartar and beat to soft peaks. Gradually beat in 3 1/2 tsp EQUAL Measure or 12 packets EQUAL sweetener, beating until stiff peaks form. Spread meringue over hot custard mixture, carefully sealing to edge of crust. Bake in preheated 425°F oven until meringue is browned, about 2 minutes. Cool on wire rack 30 minutes; refrigerate until set and chilled, about 6 hours. Cut just before serving.

Number of Servings   8

SWEET POTATO PIE

SERVING SIZE
1/8th pie

EXCHANGES
Carbohydrate   2 1/2
Fat   1 1/2

PYRAMID SERVINGS
Starch   2
Sweet   1/2
Fat   1 1/2

NUTRITION FACTS
Calories   259
Calories from Fat   79
Fat   9 g
  Saturated Fat   2 g
Cholesterol   55 mg
Sodium   400 mg
Carbohydrate   36 g
  Dietary Fiber   2 g
  Sugars   17 g
Protein   8 g

	Reduced-Fat Pie Pastry (p. 164)
2 cups	mashed cooked sweet potatoes (about 2 lb)
1 can	(12 oz) evaporated skim milk
2	eggs, lightly beaten
7 1/4 tsp	EQUAL Measure or 24 packets EQUAL sweetener or 1 cup EQUAL Spoonful
1 Tbsp	margarine, softened
1 Tbsp	all-purpose flour
1 1/2 tsp	vanilla
1 1/2–2 tsp	ground cinnamon
3/4 tsp	ground nutmeg
1/4 tsp	ground mace (optional)
1/2 tsp	salt

1. Roll pastry on floured surface into circle 1 inch larger than inverted 9-inch pie pan. Ease into pan; trim and flute edge. Blend remaining ingredients in large bowl until smooth. Pour into pastry shell.
2. Bake in preheated 425°F oven 20 minutes; reduce heat to 350°F and bake until filling is set and sharp knife inserted near center comes out clean, 30 to 35 minutes. Cool completely on wire rack; refrigerate until serving time.

Number of Servings   8

COCONUT CUSTARD PIE

SERVING SIZE
1/8th pie

EXCHANGES
Carbohydrate   1 1/2
Fat   2

PYRAMID SERVINGS
Starch   1
Sweet   1/2
Fat   2

NUTRITION FACTS
Calories   221
Calories from Fat   92
Fat   10 g
  Saturated Fat   4 g
Cholesterol   107 mg
Sodium   289 mg
Carbohydrate   24 g
  Dietary Fiber   1 g
  Sugars   9 g
Protein   8 g

	Reduced-Fat Pie Pastry (p. 164)
4	eggs
1/4 tsp	salt
2 cups	skim milk
5 1/2 tsp	EQUAL Measure or 18 packets EQUAL sweetener or 3/4 cup EQUAL Spoonful
2 tsp	coconut extract
1/2 cup	flaked coconut

1. Roll pastry on floured surface into circle 1 inch larger than inverted 9-inch pie pan. Ease into pan; trim and flute edge.
2. Beat eggs and salt in large bowl until thick and lemon-colored, about 5 minutes. Mix in milk and remaining ingredients. Pour mixture into pastry shell.
3. Bake pie in preheated 425°F oven 15 minutes. Reduce temperature to 350°F and bake until sharp knife inserted halfway between center and edge of pie comes out clean, 20 to 25 minutes. Cool on wire rack. Serve at room temperature, or refrigerate and serve chilled.

Number of Servings   8

SUMMER FRUIT TART

SERVING SIZE
1/10th recipe

EXCHANGES
Carbohydrate   1 1/2
Fat   1 1/2

PYRAMID SERVINGS
Starch   1
Fruit   1/2
Fat   1 1/2

NUTRITION FACTS
Calories   181
Calories from Fat   69
Fat   8 g
   Saturated Fat   2 g
Cholesterol   2 mg
Sodium   67 mg
Carbohydrate   26 g
   Dietary Fiber   2 g
   Sugars   10 g
Protein   3 g

1 1/4 cups	all-purpose flour
1/4 tsp	salt
1/3 cup	shortening
3–4 Tbsp	cold water
1/4 cup	plain nonfat yogurt
1/4 cup	reduced-fat dairy sour cream
1/2 tsp	EQUAL Measure or 2 packets EQUAL sweetener or 4 tsp EQUAL Spoonful
1/4 tsp	almond extract
4 cups	assorted fresh fruit
3/4 cup	pineapple juice
1 Tbsp	lemon juice
2 tsp	cornstarch
1 tsp	EQUAL Measure or 3 packets EQUAL sweetener or 2 Tbsp EQUAL Spoonful

1. Combine flour and salt; cut in shortening. Sprinkle water over mixture; toss with fork until moistened. Form into a ball.
2. Roll pastry on lightly floured surface into 10- or 11-inch circle and place in 9- or 10-inch tart pan with removable bottom. Press pastry up side; trim excess. Prick with fork. Line with foil. Bake in preheated 450°F oven 8 minutes. Remove foil; bake until golden, 5 to 6 minutes. Cool on wire rack.
3. Combine yogurt, sour cream, 1/2 tsp EQUAL Measure or 2 packets EQUAL sweetener or 4 tsp EQUAL Spoonful, and almond extract. Spread over cooled crust. Arrange fruit on top.
4. Combine pineapple juice, lemon juice, and cornstarch in small saucepan. Cook and stir until thickened and bubbly. Cook and stir 2 minutes more. Remove from heat; stir in remaining EQUAL. Cool. Spoon over fruit; cover and chill.

Number of Servings   **10**

RICH CHOCOLATE CHEESECAKE

SERVING SIZE
1/16th recipe

EXCHANGES
Carbohydrate   1
Saturated Fat   2

PYRAMID SERVINGS
Starch   1/2
Sweet   1/2
Fat   2

NUTRITION FACTS
Calories   178
Calories from Fat   100
Fat   11 g
   Saturated Fat   6 g
Cholesterol   54 mg
Sodium   316 mg
Carbohydrate   11 g
   Dietary Fiber   1 g
   Sugars   5 g
Protein   8 g

1 1/4 cups	graham cracker crumbs
4 Tbsp	margarine, melted
1 tsp	EQUAL Measure or 3 packets EQUAL sweetener or 2 Tbsp EQUAL Spoonful
2 pkg	(8 oz each) reduced-fat cream cheese, softened
1 pkg	(8 oz) fat-free cream cheese, softened
5 1/2 tsp	EQUAL Measure or 18 packets EQUAL sweetener or 3/4 cup EQUAL Spoonful
2	eggs
2	egg whites
2 Tbsp	cornstarch
1 cup	reduced-fat sour cream
1/3 cup	European or Dutch processed cocoa
1 tsp	vanilla
	Fresh mint sprigs, raspberries, nonfat whipped topping, and orange peel (optional)

1. Mix graham cracker crumbs, margarine, and 1 tsp EQUAL Measure in bottom of 9-inch springform pan. Pat mixture evenly on bottom and 1/2 inch up side of pan.
2. Beat cream cheese and 5 1/2 tsp EQUAL Measure in large bowl until fluffy; beat in eggs, egg whites and cornstarch. Mix in sour cream, cocoa, and vanilla until well blended. Pour mixture into crust.
3. Place cheesecake in roasting pan on oven rack; add 1 inch hot water to roasting pan. Bake cheesecake in preheated 300°F oven just until set in the center, 45 to

Continued

RICH CHOCOLATE CHEESECAKE *Continued*

50 minutes. Remove cheesecake from roasting pan; return cheesecake to oven. Turn oven off and let cheesecake cool 3 hours in oven with door ajar. Refrigerate 8 hours or overnight. Remove side of pan; place cheesecake on serving plate. Garnish, if desired.

Number of Servings **16**

GRANOLA BITES

SERVING SIZE
1 bite

EXCHANGES
PYRAMID SERVINGS
Starch   1/2
Fat   1/2

NUTRITION FACTS
Calories   66
Calories from Fat   18
Fat   2 g
    Saturated Fat   0 g
Cholesterol   0 mg
Sodium   61 mg
Carbohydrate   10 g
    Dietary Fiber   1 g
    Sugars   4 g
Protein   3 g

2 cups	cornflakes cereal
2/3 cup	quick-cooking oats
1/4 cup	100% bran cereal
1/2 cup	chopped pitted dates or raisins
1/2 cup	reduced-fat crunchy peanut butter
4	egg whites or 1/2 cup real liquid egg product
5 tsp	EQUAL Measure or 16 packets EQUAL sweetener or 2/3 cup EQUAL Spoonful
2 tsp	vanilla

1. Combine cornflakes, oats, bran cereal, and dates in large bowl. Mix peanut butter, egg whites, EQUAL and vanilla in small bowl until smooth; pour over cereal mixture and stir until all ingredients are coated.
2. Shape mixture into 1-inch mounds; place on lightly greased cookie sheets. Bake in preheated 350°F oven until cookies are set and browned, 8 to 10 minutes. Cool on wire racks.

Number of Servings   24

PINEAPPLE UPSIDE-DOWN CAKE

SERVING SIZE
1/8th recipe

EXCHANGES
Carbohydrate   1 1/2
Fat   1

PYRAMID SERVINGS
Starch   1
Fruit   1/2
Fat   1

NUTRITION FACTS
Calories   156
Calories from Fat   59
Fat   7 g
    Saturated Fat   1 g
Cholesterol   27 mg
Sodium   233 mg
Carbohydrate   22 g
    Dietary Fiber   1 g
    Sugars   10 g
Protein   2 g

1 can	(14 oz) unsweetened crushed pineapple in juice, undrained
1/4 cup	pecan pieces (optional)
2 Tbsp	lemon juice
1 3/4 tsp	EQUAL Measure or 6 packets EQUAL sweetener or 1/4 cup EQUAL Spoonful
1 tsp	cornstarch
4 Tbsp	margarine, at room temperature
3 1/2 tsp	EQUAL Measure or 12 packets EQUAL sweetener or 1/2 cup EQUAL Spoonful
1	egg
1 cup	cake flour
1 1/2 tsp	baking powder
1/2 tsp	baking soda
1/4 tsp	ground cinnamon
1/4 tsp	ground nutmeg
1/8 tsp	ground ginger
1/3 cup	low-fat buttermilk

1. Drain pineapple, reserving 1/4 cup juice. Mix pineapple, pecans, 1 Tbsp lemon juice, 1 3/4 tsp EQUAL Measure, and cornstarch in bottom of 8-inch square or 9-inch round cake pan; spread mixture evenly in pan.
2. Beat margarine and remaining EQUAL in medium bowl until fluffy; beat in egg. Combine flour, baking powder, baking soda, and spices in small bowl. Add to margarine mixture alternately with buttermilk, 1/4 cup reserved pineapple juice, and remaining 1 Tbsp lemon juice, beginning and ending with dry ingredients. Spread batter over pineapple mixture in cake pan.

Continued

PINEAPPLE UPSIDE-DOWN CAKE *Continued*

3. Bake in preheated 350°F oven until browned and toothpick inserted in center comes out clean, about 25 minutes. Invert cake immediately onto serving plate. Serve warm or at room temperature.

Note: If desired, maraschino cherry halves may be placed in bottom of cake pan with pineapple mixture.

Number of Servings   8

BANANA WALNUT BREAD

SERVING SIZE
1 slice

EXCHANGES
Starch   1 1/2
Fat   1

PYRAMID SERVINGS
Starch   1
Fruit   1/2
Fat   1

NUTRITION FACTS
Calories   166
Calories from Fat   59
Fat   7 g
   Saturated Fat   1 g
Cholesterol   36 mg
Sodium   270 mg
Carbohydrate   23 g
   Dietary Fiber   1 g
   Sugars   7 g
Protein   4 g

1/2 cup	skim milk
2	eggs
4 Tbsp	margarine, softened
7 1/4 tsp	EQUAL Measure or 24 packets EQUAL sweetener or 1 cup EQUAL Spoonful
1 tsp	vanilla
1/2 tsp	banana extract
1 1/4 cups	mashed ripe bananas (about 2 large)
1 3/4 cups	all-purpose flour
1 tsp	baking soda
1 tsp	ground cinnamon
1/2 tsp	salt
1/4 tsp	baking powder
1/3 cup	coarsely chopped walnuts

1. Beat milk, eggs, margarine, EQUAL, vanilla, and banana extract in large bowl with electric mixer 30 seconds; add bananas and beat on high speed 1 minute.
2. Add combined flour, baking soda, cinnamon, salt, and baking powder, mixing just until blended. Stir in walnuts. Spread mixture evenly in greased 8 1/2 x 4 1/2 x 2 1/2-inch loaf pan.
3. Bake in preheated 350°F oven until bread is golden and toothpick inserted in center comes out clean, about 60 minutes. Cool in pan on wire rack 5 minutes; remove from pan and cool on wire rack.

Makes 1 loaf (about 12 slices)
Number of Servings   12

CREAMY TAPIOCA PUDDING

SERVING SIZE
2/3 cup

EXCHANGES
Carbohydrate   1

PYRAMID SERVINGS
Starch   1/2
Milk   1/2

NUTRITION FACTS
Calories   100
Calories from Fat   13
Fat   1 g
    Saturated Fat   1 g
Cholesterol   55 mg
Sodium   184 mg
Carbohydrate   16 g
    Dietary Fiber   0 g
    Sugars   9 g
Protein   6 g

2 cups	skim milk
3 Tbsp	quick-cooking tapioca
1	egg
1/8 tsp	salt
3 1/2 tsp	EQUAL Measure or 12 packets EQUAL sweetener or 1/2 cup EQUAL Spoonful
1–2 tsp	vanilla
	Ground cinnamon and nutmeg

1. Combine milk, tapioca, egg, and salt in medium saucepan. Let stand 5 minutes. Cook over medium-high heat, stirring constantly, until boiling. Remove from heat; stir in EQUAL and vanilla.
2. Spoon mixture into serving dishes; sprinkle lightly with cinnamon and nutmeg. Serve warm, or refrigerate and serve chilled.

Number of Servings   4

BAKED VANILLA CUSTARD

SERVING SIZE
1/2 cup

EXCHANGES
Carbohydrate   1/2
Fat   1/2

PYRAMID SERVINGS
Milk   1/2

NUTRITION FACTS
Calories   89
Calories from Fat   28
Fat   3 g
  Saturated Fat   1 g
Cholesterol   129 mg
Sodium   146 mg
Carbohydrate   8 g
  Dietary Fiber   0 g
  Sugars   7 g
Protein   7 g

1 qt	skim milk
6	eggs
6 1/4 tsp	EQUAL Measure or 21 packets EQUAL sweetener or 3/4 cup + 2 Tbsp EQUAL Spoonful
2 tsp	vanilla
1/4 tsp	salt
	Ground nutmeg

1. Heat milk just to boiling in medium saucepan; let cool 5 minutes.
2. Beat eggs, EQUAL, vanilla, and salt in large bowl until smooth; gradually beat in hot milk. Pour mixture into 10 custard cups or 1 1/2-qt glass casserole; sprinkle generously with nutmeg. Place custard cups or casserole in roasting pan; add 1 inch hot water to roasting pan.
3. Bake, uncovered, in preheated 325°F oven until sharp knife inserted halfway between center and edge of custard comes out clean, 45 to 60 minutes. Remove custard dishes from roasting pan; cool on wire rack. Refrigerate until chilled.

Number of Servings   10

GRANDMA'S APPLE CRISP

SERVING SIZE
1/6th recipe

EXCHANGES
Carbohydrate   1 1/2
Fat   2

PYRAMID SERVINGS
Fruit   1
Starch   1/2
Fat   2

NUTRITION FACTS
Calories   199
Calories from Fat   92
Fat   10 g
    Saturated Fat   3 g
Cholesterol   0 mg
Sodium   91 mg
Carbohydrate   27 g
    Dietary Fiber   2 g
    Sugars   17 g
Protein   1 g

3/4 cup	apple juice
3 1/2 tsp	EQUAL Measure or 12 packets EQUAL sweetener or 1/2 cup EQUAL Spoonful
1 Tbsp	cornstarch
1 tsp	grated lemon peel
4 cups	sliced peeled apples
	Crispy Topping (recipe follows)

1. Combine apple juice, EQUAL, cornstarch, and lemon peel in medium saucepan; add apples and heat to boiling. Reduce heat and simmer, uncovered, until juice is thickened and apples begin to lose their crispness, about 5 minutes.
2. Arrange apples in 8-inch square baking pan; sprinkle Crispy Topping over apples. Bake in preheated 400°F oven until topping is browned and apples are tender, about 25 minutes. Serve warm.

CRISPY TOPPING

1/4 cup	all-purpose flour
2 1/2 tsp	EQUAL Measure or 8 packets EQUAL sweetener or 1/3 cup EQUAL Spoonful
1 tsp	ground cinnamon
1/2 tsp	ground nutmeg
3 dashes	ground allspice
4 Tbsp	cold margarine, cut into pieces
1/4 cup	quick-cooking oats
1/4 cup	unsweetened flaked coconut*

Combine flour, EQUAL, and spices in small bowl; cut in margarine with pastry blender until mixture resembles coarse crumbs. Stir in oats and coconut.

*Unsweetened coconut can be purchased in health food stores.

Number of Servings   6

FRENCH VANILLA FREEZE

SERVING SIZE
1/2 cup

EXCHANGES
Carbohydrate   1
Fat   1

PYRAMID SERVINGS
Sweet   1
Fat   1

NUTRITION FACTS
Calories   125
Calories from Fat   35
Fat   4 g
    Saturated Fat   1 g
Cholesterol   1 mg
Sodium   206 mg
Carbohydrate   14 g
    Dietary Fiber   0 g
    Sugars   11 g
Protein   7 g

10 3/4 tsp	EQUAL Measure or 36 packets EQUAL sweetener or 1 1/2 cups EQUAL Spoonful
2 Tbsp	cornstarch
1 piece	vanilla bean (2 inches)
1/8 tsp	salt
2 cups	skim milk
2 Tbsp	margarine
1 cup	real liquid egg product
1 tsp	vanilla

1. Combine EQUAL, cornstarch, vanilla bean, and salt in medium saucepan; stir in milk and margarine. Heat to boiling over medium-high heat, whisking constantly. Boil until thickened, whisking constantly, about 1 minute.
2. Whisk about 1 cup milk mixture into egg product in small bowl; whisk egg mixture back into milk mixture in saucepan. Cook over very low heat, whisking constantly, 30 to 60 seconds. Remove from heat and stir in vanilla. Let cool; remove vanilla bean. Refrigerate until chilled, about 1 hour.
3. Freeze mixture in ice cream maker according to manufacturer's directions. Pack into freezer container and freeze until firm, 8 hours or overnight. Before serving, let stand at room temperature until slightly softened, about 15 minutes.

Number of Servings   6

CREAMY RICE PUDDING

SERVING SIZE
2/3 cup

EXCHANGES
Milk, skim   1/2
Carbohydrate   2 1/2

PYRAMID SERVINGS
Starch   2 1/2
Milk   1/2

NUTRITION FACTS
Calories   242
Calories from Fat   27
Fat   3 g
   Saturated Fat   1 g
Cholesterol   109 mg
Sodium   205 mg
Carbohydrate   42 g
   Dietary Fiber   1 g
   Sugars   16 g
Protein   11 g

2 cups	water
1 stick	cinnamon, broken into pieces
1 cup	converted rice
4 cups	skim milk
1/4 tsp	salt
7 1/4 tsp	EQUAL Measure or 24 packets EQUAL sweetener or 1 cup EQUAL Spoonful
3	egg yolks
2	egg whites
1 tsp	vanilla
1/4 cup	raisins
	Ground cinnamon and nutmeg

1. Heat water and cinnamon stick to boiling in large saucepan; stir in rice. Reduce heat and simmer, covered, until rice is tender and water is absorbed, 20 to 25 minutes. Discard cinnamon stick.
2. Stir in milk and salt; heat to boiling. Reduce heat and simmer, covered, until mixture starts to thicken, about 15 to 20 minutes, stirring frequently. (Milk will not be absorbed and pudding will thicken when it cools.) Remove from heat and cool 1 to 2 minutes; stir in EQUAL.
3. Beat egg yolks, egg whites, and vanilla in small bowl until blended. Stir about 1/2 cup rice mixture into egg mixture; stir back into saucepan. Cook over low heat, stirring constantly, 1 to 2 minutes. Stir in raisins.
4. Spoon pudding into serving bowl; sprinkle with cinnamon and nutmeg. Serve warm or at room temperature.

Number of Servings   6

CHOCOLATE CRUMB PIE

SERVING SIZE
1/10th recipe

EXCHANGES
Carbohydrate   1/2
Fat   1/2

PYRAMID SERVINGS
Starch   1/2
Fat   1/2

NUTRITION FACTS
Calories   70
Calories from Fat   17
Fat   2 g
  Saturated Fat   1 g
Cholesterol   2 mg
Sodium   83 mg
Carbohydrate   10 g
  Dietary Fiber   1 g
  Sugars   3 g
Protein   3 g

6	ESTEE Fudge Cookies, crushed, divided
	Nonstick cooking spray
1 envelope	unflavored gelatin
1 3/4 cups	skim milk
1 pkg	sugar-free instant chocolate pudding and pie filling mix
1 pkg	ESTEE Whipped Topping Mix, prepared according to package directions

1. Set aside 2 Tbsp cookie crumbs. Spray pie pan with nonstick cooking spray; coat pan evenly with remaining crumbs; set aside. In small saucepan, sprinkle gelatin over 1/4 cup milk to soften. Cook over low heat until gelatin dissolves completely; remove from heat.
2. Prepare pudding according to package directions, using remaining 1 1/2 cups milk; beat in gelatin mixture. Fold in 1 cup whipped topping and spoon into prepared pan. Spread remaining whipped topping over top of pie; sprinkle reserved cookie crumbs around edges and in center of pie. Chill several hours before serving.

Number of Servings   10

LITTLE LEMON CAKES

SERVING SIZE
1 cake

EXCHANGES
Carbohydrate   2 1/2

PYRAMID SERVINGS
Starch   1 1/2
Sweet   1

NUTRITION FACTS
Calories   187
Calories from Fat   4
Fat   0 g
    Saturated Fat   0 g
Cholesterol   1 mg
Sodium   286 mg
Carbohydrate   42 g
    Dietary Fiber   1 g
    Sugars   29 g
Protein   2 g

FOR LEMON CREME:
1 pkg   instant vanilla pudding and pie
               filling mix
1 cup   skim milk
1 Tbsp   lemon juice
1 tsp   finely grated lemon rind
1 cup   ESTEE Whipped Topping,
               prepared from mix as directed

FOR CAKE:
1 pkg   fat-free lemon cake mix
1   egg white
1/2 cup   water

FOR LEMON SAUCE:
3/4 cup   cold water
1/4 cup   ESTEE Fructose
2 1/2 Tbsp   lemon juice
2 tsp   cornstarch

1. Prepare pudding according to package directions, using only 1 cup skim milk; beat in lemon juice and rind. Fold in whipped topping; cover and refrigerate.
2. Meanwhile, following package directions, prepare cupcakes using lemon cake mix, egg white, and water. While cupcakes are baking, prepare lemon sauce. In a small saucepan, combine all sauce ingredients. Cook over medium heat 5 to 7 minutes, stirring constantly until thickened; remove from heat. When cupcakes are done, cool slightly on wire rack. Using a wooden pick, poke holes in top of each cupcake. Pour 2 Tbsp lemon sauce over each cupcake. Let stand 1 hour.
3. Cut each cake in half horizontally. Spoon a dollop of lemon creme onto bottom half of each and replace top. Top with another dollop of creme.

Number of Servings   **10**

STRAWBERRY PINEAPPLE TRIFLE

SERVING SIZE
1/10th recipe

EXCHANGES
Carbohydrate   1 1/2
Fat   1/2

PYRAMID SERVINGS
Starch   1/2
Fruit   1
Fat   1/2

NUTRITION FACTS
Calories   119
Calories from Fat   24
Fat   3 g
  Saturated Fat   1 g
Cholesterol   1 mg
Sodium   70 mg
Carbohydrate   22 g
  Dietary Fiber   1 g
  Sugars   14 g
Protein   2 g

1 pkg	ESTEE Vanilla Creme-Filled Wafers
1 1/2 Tbsp	ESTEE Raspberry Fruit Spread
1 can	(20 oz) juice-packed pineapple chunks, drained, juice reserved
1 1/4 cups	skim milk
1 pkg	sugar-free instant vanilla pudding and pie filling
1 cup	ESTEE Whipped Topping, prepared from mix as directed
2 cups	sliced fresh strawberries

1. Spread one side of each wafer with fruit spread; arrange them, spread side facing in, around sides of a 1 1/2-qt souffle or trifle dish. Combine pineapple juice with skim milk. Prepare vanilla pudding according to package directions, using juice mixture instead of skim milk. Fold in whipped topping.
2. In another bowl, toss together fruit. Pour about a third of the pudding mixture in bottom of souffle dish. Top with a third of the fruit. Repeat layers, ending with fruit. Cover and refrigerate at least 1 hour before serving.

Number of Servings   10

PEACH COBBLER

SERVING SIZE
1/9th recipe

EXCHANGES
Carbohydrate   2 1/2

PYRAMID SERVINGS
Starch   1
Fruit   1/2
Sweet   1

NUTRITION FACTS
Calories   165
Calories from Fat   20
Fat   2 g
    Saturated Fat   1 g
Cholesterol   0 mg
Sodium   95 mg
Carbohydrate   36 g
    Dietary Fiber   1 g
    Sugars   26 g
Protein   2 g

*When fresh fruit is not available: In medium saucepan, combine two 16-oz cans peaches packed in juice with 1 Tbsp cornstarch. Gently stir over medium heat until mixture thickens and boils. Continue as directed.

1/3 cup	ESTEE Fructose
1 Tbsp	cornstarch
4 cups	fresh peaches, peeled, sliced (about 4 medium)*
1/2 cup	water
1 tsp	lemon juice
1 box	ESTEE Pound Cake Mix

1. Preheat oven to 375°F.
2. In medium saucepan, blend fructose and cornstarch. Stir in peaches, water, and lemon juice. Stir over medium heat until mixture thickens and boils. Pour into ungreased 1 1/2-qt casserole dish, 8 x 8 x 2 inches.
3. Keep fruit warm in oven while preparing cake batter according to package directions. Pour batter evenly over warm fruit. DO NOT STIR.
4. Bake for 25–30 minutes or until toothpick inserted in cake portion comes out clean. Serve warm and, if desired, with ESTEE Whipped Topping.

Number of Servings   9

BLUEBERRY MUFFINS

SERVING SIZE
1 muffin

EXCHANGES
Starch   1 1/2
Fat   1/2

PYRAMID SERVINGS
Starch   1
Sweet   1/2
Fat   1/2

NUTRITION FACTS
Calories   135
Calories from Fat   31
Fat   3 g
  Saturated Fat   1 g
Cholesterol   0 mg
Sodium   249 mg
Carbohydrate   24 g
  Dietary Fiber   1 g
  Sugars   11 g
Protein   3 g

1/4 cup	margarine
1/2 cup	ESTEE Fructose
2	egg whites
1/2 cup	skim milk
1/2 cup	plain, nonfat yogurt
1 1/2 cups	all-purpose flour
1 Tbsp	baking powder
1/2 tsp	salt
1 cup	blueberries, fresh or frozen, unsweetened

1. Preheat oven to 375°F.
2. Fill muffin tins with 12 paper liners. Cream margarine and fructose together. Add egg whites, skim milk, and yogurt; beat well. Mix flour, baking powder, and salt in a separate bowl, then add to fructose-egg white mixture. Beat on medium speed 3 to 4 minutes or until mixture is creamy. Fold in blueberries. Spoon batter into muffin tins and bake for 18 to 20 minutes.

Note: Additional fructose can be sprinkled on muffins before baking for a crisp topping.

Number of Servings   12

THUMBPRINT COOKIES

SERVING SIZE
3 cookies

EXCHANGES
Carbohydrate   1
Fat   1

PYRAMID SERVINGS
Starch   1
Fat   1

NUTRITION FACTS
Calories   120
Calories from Fat   71
Fat   8 g
    Saturated Fat   1 g
Cholesterol   0 mg
Sodium   33 mg
Carbohydrate   11 g
    Dietary Fiber   0 g
    Sugars   3 g
Protein   2 g

	Nonstick cooking spray
3 Tbsp	ESTEE Fructose
1 1/4 cups	all-purpose flour
1/4 tsp	ESTEE Salt-It
1 tsp	baking powder
1/2 cup	unsalted margarine
1/2 tsp	vanilla extract
1 tsp	lemon juice
1 Tbsp	orange fruit spread
1 Tbsp	water
1	egg white, slightly beaten
1/2 cup	walnuts, finely chopped
4 Tbsp	ESTEE Fruit Spread, any flavor

1. Preheat oven to 350°F. Lightly grease or spray cookie sheet with nonstick cooking spray. Mix together fructose, flour, Salt-It, and baking powder. Add margarine, vanilla extract, lemon juice, orange fruit spread, and water; mix to form a soft dough. Roll into 1-inch balls.
2. Roll each ball first in egg white, then in walnuts. Place on cookie sheet and press thumb into center of each. Bake 12 to 14 minutes; cool on wire rack. When cooled, fill each thumbprint with 1/4 tsp fruit spread.

Makes 4 dozen cookies
Number of Servings   16

191

FUDGY FRUCTOSE TOPPING

SERVING SIZE
1 Tbsp

EXCHANGES
Carbohydrate   1
Fat   1/2

PYRAMID SERVINGS
Sweet   1
Fat   1/2

NUTRITION FACTS
Calories   65
Calories from Fat   24
Fat   3 g
    Saturated Fat   1 g
Cholesterol   0 mg
Sodium   5 mg
Carbohydrate   12 g
    Dietary Fiber   0 g
    Sugars   11 g
Protein   1 g

1/2 cup	ESTEE Fructose
1 Tbsp	cornstarch
1/3 cup	skim milk
1 1/4 oz	(1/2 bar) ESTEE Dark Chocolate Bar*
1/2 tsp	vanilla
1 Tbsp	unsalted margarine

1. Mix fructose and cornstarch together, then blend with skim milk in small saucepan. Add dark chocolate bar and cook over medium heat until chocolate melts and mixture thickens and bubbles. Remove from heat.
2. Add vanilla and margarine; stir until creamy. Covers one 8- or 9-inch round or square layer cake or 10 cupcakes.

Makes 3/4 cup
Number of Servings   10

*Or substitute 1 square unsweetened chocolate, broken into small pieces.

BANANA BREAD

SERVING SIZE
1/12th recipe

EXCHANGES
Starch   2 1/2
Fat   1/2

PYRAMID SERVINGS
Starch   1
Fruit   1/2
Sweet   1
Fat   1/2

NUTRITION FACTS
Calories   204
Calories from Fat   62
Fat   7 g
   Saturated Fat   2 g
Cholesterol   0 mg
Sodium   144 mg
Carbohydrate   36 g
   Dietary Fiber   1 g
   Sugars   21 g
Protein   3 g

	Nonstick cooking spray
1 cup	ESTEE Fructose
1/2 cup	margarine
2	egg whites, slightly beaten
2 Tbsp	skim milk
3 medium	bananas, mashed
1 1/2 cups	all-purpose flour
1/4 tsp	baking soda
1/2 tsp	baking powder
1/2 tsp	ESTEE Salt-It

1. Preheat oven to 350°F. Lightly grease or spray loaf pan with nonstick cooking spray. Cream fructose and margarine. Add egg whites, skim milk, and mashed bananas. Fold in flour, baking soda, baking powder, and Salt-It. Mix well with spoon.
2. Spoon into loaf pan. Bake for 60 minutes or until toothpick inserted into center comes out clean.

Number of Servings   12

WHITE CAKE

SERVING SIZE
1/9th recipe

EXCHANGES
Carbohydrate   2 1/2
Fat   1/2

PYRAMID SERVINGS
Starch   1
Sweet   1 1/2
Fat   1/2

NUTRITION FACTS
Calories   219
Calories from Fat   70
Fat   8 g
  Saturated Fat   2 g
Cholesterol   0 mg
Sodium   213 mg
Carbohydrate   38 g
  Dietary Fiber   0 g
  Sugars   24 g
Protein   3 g

1 1/2 cups	cake flour or 1 1/4 cups all-purpose flour
1 cup	ESTEE Fructose
1 1/2 tsp	baking powder
1/2 tsp	salt
3/4 cup	skim milk
1/3 cup	shortening
2	egg whites
1 tsp	vanilla

1. Heat oven to 325°F. Grease and flour a square pan, 8 x 8 x 2 inches. Measure all ingredients into large mixing bowl. Blend 1/2 minute on low speed, scraping bowl constantly. Beat 3 minutes on high speed. Pour into pan.
2. Bake 35 to 40 minutes or until wooden pick inserted in center comes out clean. Cool on wire rack.

Number of Servings   9

FLOATING ISLANDS WITH FRESH FRUIT SAUCE

SERVING SIZE
1/6th recipe

EXCHANGES
Carbohydrate   1

PYRAMID SERVINGS
Fruit   1

NUTRITION FACTS
Calories   63
Calories from Fat   2
Fat   0 g
　Saturated Fat   0 g
Cholesterol   0 mg
Sodium   63 mg
Carbohydrate   14 g
　Dietary Fiber   2 g
　Sugars   12 g
Protein   1 g

MERINGUE
1 large   egg white
1 Tbsp   ESTEE Fructose

FRUIT SAUCE
2 cups   halved fresh or frozen straw-
　　　　　　berries
1 cup   ESTEE Raspberry Fruit Spread
1/3 cup   unsweetened orange juice
4 Tbsp   cold water, divided
1 tsp   ESTEE Fructose
2 tsp   cornstarch

To Prepare Meringue
Preheat oven to 350°F. Beat egg white until soft peaks form. Beat in fructose until egg whites are glossy and stiff. Place six mounds of whipped egg white into an 8-inch square pan filled with 1/2-inch cold water. Bake for 7 to 8 minutes, or until tops are lightly browned. Remove with slotted spoon onto waxed paper. If not using within an hour, refrigerate.

To Prepare Fruit Sauce
Place strawberries, fruit spread, orange juice, 2 Tbsp water and fructose in medium sauce pan and cook over medium heat for about 10 minutes, or until strawberries are soft. Mix remaining water with cornstarch, add to strawberry mixture and heat, stirring constantly, until thickened.

Assembly
Cool sauce and spoon into 6 individual dessert dishes or goblets. Top each with a meringue. Serve with ESTEE Strawberry or Vanilla Creme Filled Wafers. (Wafers not included in nutrient analysis.)

Number of Servings   6

195

PEACH PARFAIT PIE

SERVING SIZE
1/8th recipe

EXCHANGES
Carbohydrate   1
Fat   1

PYRAMID SERVINGS
Starch   1/2
Fruit   1/2
Fat   1

NUTRITION FACTS
Calories   119
Calories from Fat   38
Fat   4 g
   Saturated Fat   1 g
Cholesterol   2 mg
Sodium   113 mg
Carbohydrate   18 g
   Dietary Fiber   1 g
   Sugars   9 g
Protein   2 g

CRUST

6	ESTEE Vanilla Flavor Cookies, crushed
8	graham crackers, crushed
1/2 tsp	allspice
2 Tbsp	reduced-calorie margarine, melted
2 Tbsp	nonfat plain yogurt

FILLING

1 pkg	sugar-free peach melba gelatin mix
1 can	(16 oz) juice-packed sliced peaches, drained, reserve juice
1 pkg	ESTEE Whipped Topping Mix

To Prepare Crust
Heat oven to 400°F. In 9-inch pie pan, combine cookie and cracker crumbs with allspice. Stir in margarine and yogurt. Pat into bottom and up sides of pie pan. Bake 8 to 10 minutes or until browned; remove and cool on rack.

To Prepare Filling
Meanwhile, combine gelatin mix with 1 cup boiling water, stirring until dissolved. Add 3/4 cup cold water and reserved peach juice to gelatin mixture. Refrigerate 1 hour or until slightly thickened. Meanwhile, reserve 8 peach slices for garnish; chop remaining peaches and set aside. Prepare whipped topping according to package directions. Fold 1 cup whipped topping and chopped peaches into chilled gelatin. Spoon into prepared crust. Chill remaining whipped topping. Chill pie about 1 1/2 hours until firm, or freeze several hours if desired. To serve, pipe remaining whipped topping around border of pie and garnish with reserved peach slices.

Number of Servings   8

APPLE CRISP DESSERT

SERVING SIZE
1/6th recipe

EXCHANGES
Carbohydrate   2
Fat   1 1/2

PYRAMID SERVINGS
Starch   1/2
Fruit   1/2
Sweet   1
Fat   1 1/2

NUTRITION FACTS
Calories   200
Calories from Fat   70
Fat   8 g
  Saturated Fat   1 g
Cholesterol   0 mg
Sodium   19 mg
Carbohydrate   34 g
  Dietary Fiber   2 g
  Sugars   22 g
Protein   1 g

	Nonstick cooking spray
4 cups	apples, sliced and pared (about 4 medium)
1/4 cup	ESTEE Fructose
18	ESTEE Oatmeal Raisin Cookies
2 Tbsp	unsalted margarine, softened
1 tsp	cinnamon

1. Preheat oven to 375°F. Spray 8- or 9-inch square baking pan with nonstick coating.
2. Toss apple slices with fructose to coat evenly; spread in pan.
3. Using food processor or blender, process cookies into fine crumbs (enough to make 1 cup). Mix crumbs, margarine, and cinnamon together with fork until crumbly. Sprinkle topping evenly over fruit. Bake for 20 to 30 minutes or until apples are tender. Serve warm or cold.

Number of Servings   6

MULTI-GRAIN APPLE RAISIN MUFFINS

SERVING SIZE
1 muffin

EXCHANGES
Carbohydrate   1 1/2
Fat   1/2

PYRAMID SERVINGS
Starch   1
Fruit   1/2
Fat   1/2

NUTRITION FACTS
Calories   146
Calories from Fat   37
Fat   4 g
    Saturated Fat   1 g
Cholesterol   0 mg
Sodium   29 mg
Carbohydrate   26 g
    Dietary Fiber   2 g
    Sugars   12 g
Protein   4 g

2 cups	GRAINFIELD's Multi-Grain Flakes
1 1/4 cups	skim milk
1 cup	whole wheat flour or all-purpose flour
2 1/2 tsp	low-sodium baking powder
1/2 tsp	nutmeg (optional)
1/2 cup	chopped apple
1/2 cup	raisins
2	egg whites, slightly beaten
3 Tbsp	vegetable oil
1/4 cup	honey or equivalent sugar substitute
2 tsp	vanilla

1. Mix Multi-Grain Flakes and skim milk. Let stand 5 minutes. Blend flour, baking powder, and nutmeg into cereal mixture. Set aside.
2. In small bowl, with a wire whisk, stir egg whites, oil, honey, and vanilla until well blended and frothy. Stir into cereal-flour mixture until moistened. Stir in apples and raisins.
3. Heat oven to 400°F. Line 12 medium muffin cups with paper baking cups. Fill 2/3 full. Bake 15 to 20 minutes, or until golden brown.

Number of Servings   12

QUICKBREAD

SERVING SIZE
1 slice

EXCHANGES
Carbohydrate   1 1/2

PYRAMID SERVINGS
Starch   1
Sweet   1/2

NUTRITION FACTS
Calories   128
Calories from Fat   25
Fat   3 g
    Saturated Fat   1 g
Cholesterol   11 mg
Sodium   59 mg
Carbohydrate   25 g
    Dietary Fiber   1 g
    Sugars   14 g
Protein   2 g

1 cup	skim milk
1 1/2 cups	flour
2/3 cup	honey
2 1/2 tsp	baking powder
1	egg, beaten
1/4 cup	molasses
1/4 cup	unsalted butter or margarine, melted and cooled
3 cups	GRAINFIELD's Low-Sodium Raisin Bran

1. Soften cereal in milk. Sift dry ingredients. Stir egg, molasses, honey, and butter into softened cereal. Add flour mixture and stir just to moisten all flour.
2. Pour into greased 9 x 5-inch loaf pan (or 2 smaller pans). Bake at 325°F for approximately one hour. Cool in pan for 10 minutes. Remove and finish cooling on rack.
3. Other dried fruits can be added. Serve plain or with whipped cream or hot unsweetened applesauce.

Number of Servings   20

CAROB TREATS

SERVING SIZE
1 square

EXCHANGES
Carbohydrate   1/2
Monounsat Fat   1/2

PYRAMID SERVINGS
Sweet   1/2
Fat   1/2

NUTRITION FACTS
Calories   65
Calories from Fat   32
Fat   4 g
    Saturated Fat   1 g
Cholesterol   0 mg
Sodium   9 mg
Carbohydrate   7 g
    Dietary Fiber   1 g
    Sugars   4 g
Protein   2 g

1 cup	carob morsels
1/2 cup	natural peanut butter
1/4 cup	honey or maple syrup
3 cups	GRAINFIELD's Brown Rice

1. Melt carob morsels, peanut butter, and honey or maple syrup together in large saucepan over very low heat. Stir constantly until smooth.
2. Remove from heat and add GRAINFIELD's Brown Rice. Stir until well coated. Press mixture evenly into buttered 9 x 9 x 2-inch pan. Chill until firm. Cut into 1-inch squares.

Number of Servings   36

FRUIT CRUMBLE COOKIES

SERVING SIZE
1 cookie

EXCHANGES
Carbohydrate   1/2
Fat   1

PYRAMID SERVINGS
Fruit   1/2
Fat   1

NUTRITION FACTS
Calories   78
Calories from Fat   37
Fat   4 g
   Saturated Fat   1 g
Cholesterol   0 mg
Sodium   34 mg
Carbohydrate   10 g
   Dietary Fiber   1 g
   Sugars   5 g
Protein   1 g

1 cup	sifted whole wheat flour
1 cup	GRAINFIELD's Multi-Grain Flakes With Rice Bran, crushed
3/4 cup	margarine or oil
3	egg whites, or 1/2 cup egg substitute
2 tsp	vanilla
2 tsp	low-sodium baking powder
1 1/2 cups	chopped dates
1 1/2 cups	chopped (unsulfured) dried apricots
1 cup	unsalted walnuts

1. Bring margarine to room temperature. In small bowl, beat margarine, egg whites, and vanilla together until smooth. Mix flour, baking powder, Multi-Grain Flakes and add to creamed margarine mixture. Mix until well blended. Add fruits and nuts and mix well.

2. Form dough into two 2-inch rolls. Wrap in waxed paper or foil. Chill in the freezer until firm enough to slice (or place in refrigerator overnight). Cut with a sharp wet knife into 3/8-inch-thick slices. Place slices on lightly oiled baking sheet and bake in preheated 350°F oven about 10 to 12 minutes, or until golden brown. Cool on wire rack.

Note: If desired, cookies may be formed into small balls without chilling dough. Flatten slightly before baking.

Number of Servings   48

RAISIN BRAN APPLESAUCE COOKIES

SERVING SIZE
1 3-inch cookie

EXCHANGES
Carbohydrate   1
Fat   1/2

PYRAMID SERVINGS
Starch   1/2
Sweet   1/2
Fat   1/2

NUTRITION FACTS
Calories   96
Calories from Fat   34
Fat   4 g
   Saturated Fat   1 g
Cholesterol   4 mg
Sodium   16 mg
Carbohydrate   15 g
   Dietary Fiber   1 g
   Sugars   7 g
Protein   2 g

2 1/2 cups	flour
1 3/4 tsp	unsalted baking powder
1 tsp	cinnamon
1/2 Tbsp	nutmeg
1/2 cup	unsalted butter or margarine
1 cup	honey or maple syrup
1	egg
1 cup	applesauce
1 cup	chopped nuts
4 cups	GRAINFIELD's Raisin Bran

1. Stir together dry ingredients. Set aside in large mixing bowl.
2. Beat margarine and hone until well blended. Add egg, beating well. Add flour mixture and GRAINFIELD's Raisin Bran alternating with applesauce. Stir in nuts.
3. Drop onto a greased cookie sheet. Bake at 350°F for 15–17 minutes.

Number of Servings   48

GRANOLA BARS

SERVING SIZE
1/24th recipe

EXCHANGES
Carbohydrate   1
Polyunsat Fat   1 1/2

PYRAMID SERVINGS
Starch   1/2
Sweet   1/2
Fat   1 1/2

NUTRITION FACTS
Calories   153
Calories from Fat   77
Fat   9 g
    Saturated Fat   1 g
Cholesterol   9 mg
Sodium   6 mg
Carbohydrate   18 g
    Dietary Fiber   1 g
    Sugars   11 g
Protein   2 g

3/4 cup	honey or maple syrup
1/2 cup	oil
1	egg, beaten
2 Tbsp	skim milk
1 1/4 cups	oatmeal
1/2 cup	flour
1 tsp	cinnamon
1/2 cup	walnuts
1/2 cup	sesame seeds
1/2 cup	mixed dried fruit
1 1/2 cups	GRAINFIELD's Corn Flakes

1. Blend honey, oil, and egg. Stir in milk, oatmeal, flour, GRAINFIELD's Corn Flakes, cinnamon, nuts, seeds, and dried fruit. Dough should be stiff. Drop by tablespoons onto greased cookie sheet. Shape into bars.
2. Bake at 375°F for 12 minutes.

Number of Servings   24

CARROT HONEY OAT BRAN MUFFINS

SERVING SIZE
1 muffin

EXCHANGES
Carbohydrate   2
Fat   1/2

PYRAMID SERVINGS
Starch   1
Sweet   1
Fat   1/2

NUTRITION FACTS
Calories   174
Calories from Fat   32
Fat   4 g
    Saturated Fat   1 g
Cholesterol   0 mg
Sodium   59 mg
Carbohydrate   34 g
    Dietary Fiber   3 g
    Sugars   19 g
Protein   4 g

1/4 cup	(or 1/2 stick) margarine, melted (or substitute oil)
3/4 cup	honey
3/4 cup	skim or low-fat milk
3	egg whites, or 3/4 cup egg substitute
1 Tbsp	finely grated orange peel
1 Tbsp	orange juice
1 1/4 cups	whole wheat flour
2 cups	GRAINFIELD's Oat Bran Flakes crushed
2 1/2 Tbsp	low-sodium baking powder
1 cup	grated carrots
1 1/2 tsp	nutmeg
1 tsp	cinnamon
1/2 cup	raisins

1. Pour milk over crushed oat bran. Let sit 10 minutes. In saucepan, melt margarine with honey. Remove from heat, stir in egg whites, orange peel, and orange juice. Set aside.
2. Add oat bran mixture and stir until mixed. Stir in grated carrots and raisins.
3. Bake in well-oiled muffin tins at 375°F until done, about 15 minutes. Tops should spring back when touched. These muffins can be frozen and/or reheated.

Number of Servings   15

CINNAMON APPLESAUCE BREAD

SERVING SIZE
1 slice

EXCHANGES
Carbohydrate   1 1/2

PYRAMID SERVINGS
Starch   1
Sweet   1/2

NUTRITION FACTS
Calories   110
Calories from Fat   20
Fat   2 g
    Saturated Fat   0 g
Cholesterol   10 mg
Sodium   130 mg
Carbohydrate   22 g
    Dietary Fiber   1 g
    Sugars   11 g
Protein   2 g

1 1/2 cups	flour
1 Tbsp	CALUMET Baking Powder
1 1/2 tsp	ground cinnamon
1/4 tsp	salt
1	egg
1 cup	chunky applesauce, unsweetened
3/4 cup	firmly packed brown sugar
2/3 cup	skim milk
2 Tbsp	oil
1 1/2 cups	POST Bran Flakes
1/4 cup	chopped walnuts (optional)
	Nonstick cooking spray

1. Heat oven to 350°F.
2. Mix flour, baking powder, cinnamon, and salt in large bowl. Beat egg in small bowl; stir in applesauce, sugar, milk, and oil. Add to flour mixture; stir just until moistened. (Batter will be lumpy.) Stir in cereal and walnuts. Pour into 9 x 5-inch loaf pan which has been sprayed with nonstick cooking spray.
3. Bake 55 minutes or until toothpick inserted in center comes out clean. Cool 10 minutes; remove from pan. Cool completely on wire rack.

Note: For easier slicing, wrap bread and store overnight.

Number of Servings   ***18 (1/2-inch thick) slices***

Reprinted with permission of Kraft Foods, Inc.

APPLESAUCE YOGURT DELIGHT

SERVING SIZE
1/2 cup

EXCHANGES
Carbohydrate   1/2

PYRAMID SERVINGS
Sweet   1

NUTRITION FACTS
Calories   60
Calories from Fat   0
Fat   0 g
    Saturated Fat   0 g
Cholesterol   3 mg
Sodium   90 mg
Carbohydrate   10 g
    Dietary Fiber   1 g
    Sugars   9 g
Protein   3 g

1 cup	boiling water
1 pkg	(4-serving size) JELL-O Brand Sugar Free Low Calorie Gelatin Dessert, any red flavor
3/4 cup	chilled applesauce, unsweetened
1/4 tsp	ground cinnamon
1/2 cup	BREYERS Vanilla Lowfat Yogurt

1. Stir boiling water into gelatin in medium bowl at least 2 minutes until completely dissolved. Measure 3/4 cup; stir in applesauce and cinnamon. Pour into bowl or 4 dessert glasses. Refrigerate until set but not firm.
2. Refrigerate remaining gelatin until slightly thickened. Mix in yogurt; spoon over gelatin in bowl.
3. Refrigerate 2 hours or until set.

Number of Servings   4

Reprinted with permission of Kraft Foods, Inc.

CHOCOLATE BANANA SPLIT

SERVING SIZE
1/4th recipe

EXCHANGES
Carbohydrate   2

PYRAMID SERVINGS
Starch   1/2
Fruit   1
Milk   1/2

NUTRITION FACTS
Calories   160
Calories from Fat   25
Fat   3 g
    Saturated Fat   1.5 g
Cholesterol   2 mg
Sodium   380 mg
Carbohydrate   29 g
    Dietary Fiber   2 g
    Sugars   16 g
Protein   6 g

2 cups	cold skim milk
1 pkg	(4-serving size) JELL-O Chocolate Flavor Fat Free Sugar Free Instant Reduced Calorie Pudding & Pie Filling
2 medium	bananas, sliced
1/2 cup	thawed COOL WHIP LITE Whipped Topping
1 Tbsp	chopped walnuts

1. Pour milk into medium bowl. Add pudding mix. Beat with wire whisk 2 minutes.
2. Spoon 1/2 of the pudding evenly into 4 dessert dishes. Layer with banana slices. Spoon remaining pudding over bananas.
3. Refrigerate until ready to serve. Top each serving with 2 Tbsp whipped topping. Sprinkle with walnuts. Store leftover dessert in refrigerator.

Number of Servings   4

Reprinted with permission of Kraft Foods, Inc.

FRESH FRUIT PARFAITS

SERVING SIZE
1/6th recipe

EXCHANGES
Carbohydrate   1/2

PYRAMID SERVINGS
Fruit   1/2

NUTRITION FACTS
Calories   35
Calories from Fat   10
Fat   1 g
   Saturated Fat   1 g
Cholesterol   0 mg
Sodium   55 mg
Carbohydrate   5 g
   Dietary Fiber   1 g
   Sugars   3 g
Protein   1 g

1/2 cup	strawberries, sliced
1/2 cup	blueberries
3/4 cup	boiling water
1 pkg	(4-serving size) JELL-O Brand Sugar Free Low Calorie Gelatin Dessert, any flavor
1/2 cup	cold water
	Ice cubes
3/4 cup	thawed COOL WHIP LITE Whipped Topping

1. Divide fruit among 6 dessert glasses.
2. Stir boiling water into gelatin in medium bowl at least 2 minutes until completely dissolved. Mix cold water and ice cubes to make 1 1/4 cups. Add to gelatin, stirring until slightly thickened. Remove any remaining ice. Measure 3/4 cup of the gelatin; pour into dessert glasses. Refrigerate 1 hour or until set but not firm (should stick to finger when touched and should mound).
3. Stir whipped topping into remaining gelatin with wire whisk until smooth. Spoon over gelatin in glasses.
4. Refrigerate 1 hour or until firm. Store left-over parfaits in refrigerator.

Number of Servings   6

Reprinted with permission of Kraft Foods, Inc.

FRUITY MOUSSE

SERVING SIZE
1/2 cup

EXCHANGES
Carbohydrate   1/2
Saturated Fat   1/2

PYRAMID SERVINGS
Sweet   1/2
Fat   1/2

NUTRITION FACTS
Calories   80
Calories from Fat   30
Fat   3 g
    Saturated Fat   3 g
Cholesterol   3 mg
Sodium   130 mg
Carbohydrate   9 g
    Dietary Fiber   0 g
    Sugars   6 g
Protein   5 g

1 pkg	(8 oz) PHILADELPHIA BRAND FREE Fat Free Cream Cheese, softened
1 tub	CRYSTAL LIGHT Pink Lemonade Flavor Low Calorie Soft Drink Mix, divided
1 cup	skim milk
1 tub	(8 oz) COOL WHIP LITE Whipped Topping, thawed

1. Beat cream cheese and 1 1/2 tsp of the drink mix in large bowl with electric mixer on medium speed until well blended and smooth. Gradually add milk, mixing until well blended.
2. Gently stir in whipped topping until well blended. Pour into serving bowl or individual dishes.
3. Refrigerate 3 hours or until firm. Serve with fresh fruit, if desired.

Note: Place remaining drink mix in glass or plastic pitcher. Add 1 quart water; stir to dissolve. Serve over ice.

Number of Servings   10

Reprinted with permission of Kraft Foods, Inc.

LEMON SOUFFLE CHEESECAKE

SERVING SIZE
1/8th recipe

EXCHANGES
Carbohydrate   1
Saturated Fat   2

PYRAMID SERVINGS
Fruit   1/2
Sweet   1/2
Fat   2

NUTRITION FACTS
Calories   150
Calories from Fat   70
Fat   7 g
    Saturated Fat   5 g
Cholesterol   20 mg
Sodium   280 mg
Carbohydrate   14 g
    Dietary Fiber   2 g
    Sugars   10 g
Protein   8 g

	Nonstick cooking spray
1	graham cracker, crushed or 2 Tbsp graham cracker crumbs, divided
1 pkg	(4-serving size) JELL-O Brand Lemon Flavor Sugar Free Low Calorie Gelatin Dessert
2/3 cup	boiling water
1 cup	LIGHT N' LIVELY 1% Lowfat Cottage Cheese
1 container	(8 oz) PHILADELPHIA LIGHT Cream Cheese
2 cups	thawed COOL WHIP LITE Whipped Topping
1 pint	strawberries, sliced
2	kiwi, peeled and sliced

1. Sprinkle 1/2 of the crumbs onto sides of 8- or 9-inch springform pan or 9-inch pie plate that has been sprayed with nonstick cooking spray.*
2. Completely dissolve gelatin in boiling water. Pour into blender container. Add cheeses; cover. Blend on medium speed until smooth, scraping down sides occasionally.
3. Pour into large bowl. Gently stir in whipped topping. Pour into prepared pan; smooth top. Sprinkle remaining crumbs around outside edge. Refrigerate 4 hours or until set.
4. Remove side of pan just before serving. Arrange fruit on top of cheesecake.

Number of Servings   8

*If desired, omit graham cracker crumb garnish; sprinkle bottom of pan with remaining crumbs.

Reprinted with permission of Kraft Foods, Inc.

LOW FAT BLUEBERRY MUFFINS

SERVING SIZE
1 muffin

EXCHANGES
Carbohydrate   2

PYRAMID SERVINGS
Starch   1
Fruit   1/2
Sweet   1/2

NUTRITION FACTS
Calories   160
Calories from Fat   25
Fat   2.5 g
    Saturated Fat   0.5 g
Cholesterol   20 mg
Sodium   280 mg
Carbohydrate   31 g
    Dietary Fiber   2 g
    Sugars   13 g
Protein   4 g

1 1/4 cups	flour
1 Tbsp	CALUMET Baking Powder
1 tsp	ground cinnamon
1/2 tsp	salt
1 cup	POST GRAPE-NUTS Cereal
1 cup	skim milk
1	egg, slightly beaten
1/2 cup	chunky applesauce, unsweetened
1/2 cup	firmly packed brown sugar
2 Tbsp	margarine, melted
1 cup	fresh or frozen blueberries
	Nonstick cooking spray

1. Heat oven to 400°F.
2. Mix flour, baking powder, cinnamon, and salt in large bowl. Mix cereal and milk in another bowl; let stand 3 minutes. Stir in egg, applesauce, sugar, and margarine. Add to flour mixture; stir just until moistened. (Batter will be lumpy.) Stir in blueberries. Spoon batter into muffin pan that has been sprayed with nonstick cooking spray, filling each cup 2/3 full.
3. Bake 20 minutes or until golden brown. Serve warm.

Storage: Store muffins loosely covered at room temperature on the day they are baked. For longer storage, wrap tightly and freeze. Defrost frozen muffins, loosely covered, at room temperature 1 hour; then warm in 350°F oven several minutes before serving.

Number of Servings   12

SPARKLING LEMON ICE

SERVING SIZE
1/6th recipe

EXCHANGES
PYRAMID SERVINGS
Free Food

NUTRITION FACTS
Calories   10
Calories from Fat   0
Fat   0 g
   Saturated Fat   0 g
Cholesterol   0 mg
Sodium   50 mg
Carbohydrate   1 g
   Dietary Fiber   0 g
   Sugars   0 g
Protein   1 g

1 pkg	(4-serving size) JELL-O Brand Lemon Flavor Sugar Free Low Calorie Gelatin Dessert
1 cup	boiling water
1 cup	chilled lemon-lime–flavored seltzer
3 Tbsp	fresh lemon juice
1/2 tsp	grated lemon peel

1. Stir boiling water into gelatin in medium bowl 2 minutes until completely dissolved. Stir in seltzer, lemon juice, and peel. Pour into 9-inch square pan; cover.
2. Freeze 3 hours or until frozen. Let stand at room temperature 10 minutes.
3. Beat with electric mixer or blend in covered blender container on high speed until smooth. Spoon into dessert dishes. Store leftover ice in freezer.

Number of Servings   6

Reprinted with permission of Kraft Foods, Inc.

WHITE CHOCOLATE DEVIL'S FOOD PIE

SERVING SIZE
1/8th recipe

EXCHANGES
Carbohydrate   3
Saturated Fat   1

PYRAMID SERVINGS
Sweet   3
Fat   1

NUTRITION FACTS
Calories   280
Calories from Fat 60
Fat   7 g
  Saturated Fat   4.5 g
Cholesterol   0 mg
Sodium   490 mg*
Carbohydrate   50 g
  Dietary Fiber   0.5 g
  Sugars   33 g
Protein   4 g

2 cups	cold skim milk, divided
1 pkg	(4-serving size) JELL-O Devil's Food Flavor Fat Free Instant Pudding & Pie Filling
1 tub	(8 oz) thawed COOL WHIP LITE Whipped Topping, divided
1 (6 oz)	prepared reduced fat graham cracker crumb crust
1 pkg	(4-serving size) JELL-O White Chocolate Flavor Fat Free Instant Pudding & Pie Filling

1. Pour 1 cup of the cold milk into medium bowl. Add devil's food flavor pudding mix. Beat with wire whisk 1 minute. (Mixture will be thick.) Gently stir in 1/2 of the whipped topping. Spoon evenly into crust.
2. Pour remaining 1 cup cold milk into another medium bowl. Add white choco-late flavor pudding mix. Beat with wire whisk 1 minute. (Mixture will be thick.) Gently stir in remaining whipped topping. Spread over pudding layer in crust.
3. Refrigerate 4 hours or until set. Garnish with additional whipped topping, if desired. Store leftover pie in refrigerator.

Number of Servings   8

* >400 mg of sodium

Reprinted with permission of Kraft Foods, Inc.

SCALLOPED APPLE BAKE

SERVING SIZE
1/10th recipe

EXCHANGES
Carbohydrate   2 1/2
Monounsat Fat   1 1/2

PYRAMID SERVINGS
Starch   1/2
Fruit   1
Sweet   1
Fat   1 1/2

NUTRITION FACTS
Calories   235
Calories from Fat   76
Fat   8 g
  Saturated Fat   1 g
Cholesterol   0 mg
Sodium   163 mg
Carbohydrate   41 g
  Dietary Fiber   3 g
  Sugars   31 g
Protein   1 g

1/4 cup	margarine or butter, melted
1/4 cup	sugar
2 tsp	grated orange peel
1 tsp	ground cinnamon
1 1/2 cups	PEPPERIDGE FARM Corn Bread Stuffing
1/2 cup	coarsely chopped pecans
1 can	(16 oz) whole berry cranberry sauce
1/3 cup	orange juice or water
4 large	cooking apples, cored and thinly sliced (about 6 cups)

1. Lightly mix margarine, sugar, orange peel, cinnamon, stuffing, and pecans. Set aside.
2. Mix cranberry sauce, juice, and apples. Add half of stuffing mixture. Mix lightly. Spoon into 8-inch square baking dish. Sprinkle remaining stuffing mixture over apple mixture.
3. Bake at 375°F for 40 minutes or until apples are tender.

Number of Servings   10

Recipe provided courtesy of Campbell Soup Company.

BANANA-NANA SPLIT PIE

SERVING SIZE
1/12th recipe

EXCHANGES
Carbohydrate   2
Fat 1

PYRAMID SERVINGS
Starch   1
Sweet   1
Fat   1

NUTRITION FACTS
Calories   179
Calories from Fat   62
Fat   7 g
   Saturated Fat   3 g
Cholesterol   11 mg
Sodium   75 mg
Carbohydrate   26 g
   Dietary Fiber   1 g
   Sugars   12 g
Protein   4 g

1 8-inch	chocolate cookie crust
1 medium	banana, mashed
4 1/2 cups	ESKIMO PIE Reduced-Fat, sweetened with NUTRASWEET, vanilla ice cream
3/4 cup	fresh sliced berries to garnish Lite nondairy topping

Let ice cream soften. Stir in banana. Spoon mixture into cookie crust. Cover. Freeze for 12 hours or more. Top with fresh berries and 12 Tbsp of nondairy topping. Slice frozen.

Number of Servings   12

SOUTHERN PEACHY PARFAIT

SERVING SIZE
1 parfait

EXCHANGES
Carbohydrate   2
Saturated fat 1/2

PYRAMID SERVINGS
Starch   1
Fruit   1/2
Sweet   1/2
Fat   1/2

NUTRITION FACTS
Calories   161
Calories from Fat   42
Fat   5 g
   Saturated Fat   3 g
Cholesterol   15 mg
Sodium   37 mg
Carbohydrate   28 g
   Dietary Fiber   1 g
   Sugars   14 g
Protein   5 g

6	parfait glasses
3 cups	ESKIMO PIE Reduced-Fat, sweetened with NUTRASWEET, ice cream (Vanilla or Butter Pecan)
6	lowfat cinnamon graham cracker squares, crushed
1 1/2 cups	fresh sliced peaches or canned peaches (packed in juice) or fresh berries
	Lite nondairy topping

Place 1/4 cup of ice cream in each parfait glass. Top with 1/6 of crushed crumbs. Then add 1–2 Tbsp of fresh fruit. Layer with 1/4 cup ice cream. Freeze until ready to serve. Garnish with 1 Tbsp of fresh fruit and 1 Tbsp of nondairy topping.

Number of Servings   6

IGLOO CAKE

SERVING SIZE
1/9th recipe

EXCHANGES
Carbohydrate   1 1/2
Saturated fat 1/2

PYRAMID SERVINGS
Starch   1
Sweet   1/2
Fat   1/2

NUTRITION FACTS
Calories   146
Calories from Fat   40
Fat   4 g
    Saturated Fat   3 g
Cholesterol   7 mg
Sodium   74 mg
Carbohydrate   23 g
    Dietary Fiber   1 g
    Sugars   5 g
Protein   3 g

1 box	ESKIMO PIE Reduced-Fat No-Sugar-Added sandwiches
2 cups	Lite nondairy topping
3/4 cup	sliced strawberries or other fresh fruit (blueberries, peaches)

Unwrap 3 sandwiches. Place side by side on large plate to form a rectangle. Top with 1/2 cup of nondairy topping. Unwrap last 3 sandwiches and place on top of nondairy topping. Ice top and sides of sandwiches with nondairy topping. Freeze for 1 hour or longer. Spread berries over top of cake. Cut while frozen.

Variation: Igloo Birthday Cake
Prepare as above, eliminate the strawberries. Top with 1 Tbsp of colored sprinkles.

Variation: Animal Zoo Party Cake
Prepare as above, eliminate food decorations. Decorate top and sides with 20 animal crackers or teddy bear graham crackers.

Number of Servings   9

ANGEL DELIGHT

SERVING SIZE
1 angel delight

EXCHANGES
Carbohydrate   2
Saturated fat 1/2

PYRAMID SERVINGS
Starch   1
Fruit   1/2
Sweet   1/2
Fat   1/2

NUTRITION FACTS
Calories   158
Calories from Fat   25
Fat   3 g
  Saturated Fat   2 g
Cholesterol   8 mg
Sodium   55 mg
Carbohydrate   30 g
  Dietary Fiber   2 g
  Sugars   16 g
Protein   4 g

One	1-inch wedge Angel Food Cake (store bought)
1/4 cup	ESKIMO PIE Reduced-Fat, sweetened with NUTRASWEET, ice cream (any flavor)
1/2 cup	fresh berries or 1/4 cup sliced peaches
1 Tbsp	Lite nondairy topping

Top wedge of cake with ice cream, sprinkle with fruit, and top with nondairy topping.

Number of Servings   1

Index